BUSINESS MODEL

SIMPLIFIES WITH EXAMPLES FROM GLOBAL COMPANIES

By
DR. FIREND ALAN RASCH

1

Table of Content

Introduction

Companies and society has always been the rubric that holds the very make up of business activities. Combined, these two forces form the essence of contribution to what makes economy, shaping our daily activities, and the formation of business cycles. Given the ever-increasing complexity of the global marketplace, business (exchange of good and services, manufacturing, farming, production, distribution, sales and consumption) is rooted in the way we live and how our societies and ultimately nations, progress. A viable, efficient and effective business model is vital to organizational success of failure. Business model is not just a theme of focus when reacting to a crisis, or simply the operational structure of a given enterprise. Business model is the manifestation of the very existence of the organization, business, firm, group, agency, governmental department or a person with a purpose of providing a service to others.

This book attempts to provide numerous examples of companies from around the world, to show how various entities are operating and shaping the global economy. To fully comprehend such themes into practice, one need to look at various market players by examining how they structure their operations and conduct everyday tasks in pursuit of their objectives. This book analyses numerous companies' business modules, and attempts to illustrate to the reader the varying operational mechanism that makes them succeed. Business models of some big name companies have been examined here to illustrate how big as well as small firms, structure themselves to provide solutions of value to others. The cases in this book also detail the strategies (actions) [1] taken that contributes to the success of the firm and ultimately, reshaping the business model altogether. The biggest lesson to mention here is that companies must constantly change their business model to survive in the marketplace. Those who don't manage to evolve their business models, or reinvent themselves, are doomed to become extinct and irrelevant. Those who do not manage to change their business model to remain relevant to their marketplace and consumers; they disappear and get replaced by others with more relevance to the consumer needs. For example, Kaiser was the largest ship builder in the U.S.A. during World-War II, today they are one of the top five health insurance companies. Tesla was one of the first electric car manufacturers. Slowly, they are shifting to electric energy providers rather than just electric car company. Uber started as an intermediary between drivers and passengers, now they are redefining the concept of transportation. These companies understand the importance of redefining their business models constantly to remain relevant, by venturing into new unsaturated areas of consumer demand. While the reader gets the opportunity of examining various business models, let it not escape your attention as to how these businesses need to further restructure their business models to maintain future competitive advantage.

What is Business Model?

Different people define the concept of business model differently. For the average person, business model merely describes the way in which a firm makes money (Krehmeyer, 2012). Peter Drucker (1994) coined the concept by describing it initially as the "theory of business". Some see it as the company plan for generating revenues, some see it as the structure of operations and how to organize various activities to provide services, others define it as the architecture of the organization and division of resources to generate profits. Michael Lewis refers to the phrase business model as "a term of art" (Ovans, 2015). All are adequate views of what a business model is. I however, tend to favor Thompson et. al. (2013) interpretation of what business model is, which they describe as being value proposition and a profit formula. The value proposition consists of satisfying consumer's wants and needs through value offering to generate profits.

A business model can be simple or complex. For example, a restaurant business model is to generate revenues by cooking and serving food to hungry customers. A production business model might not be so simple, as there are many ways in which companies can generate revenue. On the other hand, a fashion or an electronic company may need to keep changing their model to survive with the changing consumer needs and wants in addition to changing market conditions and requirements. Such changing conditions are highly impacted by evolution in technology, which is causing rapid disruption to all existing business models. The business model diagrams in the next pages explain this idea. Cases in this book don't stop at highlighting the business model only, but explains both factors that contribute to the success of a given company and the challenges they face. In fact, one of the most valuable lessons I learned from my consulting days is that what triggers the stagnant conditions of so many large and successful organizations is that their business model is no longer viable.

Every organization then, big or small has a theory of their own business existence. Some are very successful by being conscious of their business structure and adjust their resources and strategies according to changing demands and market conditions. While others are less successful because either they fail to understand their market (consumer demands, market segment, wants or needs to serve, impact of regulations, globalization, technology, or emerging changes in their environment), or they failed to compete, primarily because of errors in human judgment (management and/or personnel).

Most importantly, failing to adapt their business model to accommodate constant changes in the variables described earlier. Since everything is subject to change, business models must evolve overtime and change to accommodate changes that affects the business. As simple as it may sound, most companies large or small tends to go through a long process of trial and error, to get their business model right. For those who get it right the first time by determining an urgent need and fulfill an existing demand while generating profits, they cannot escape the point of saturation and decline in their business. Hence, they need to re-examine the variables described above that makes up their business model, and strive to redesign it in a way that give them a competitive advantage and more relevance to consumer needs. As we approach the forth-industrial revolution of Artificial Intelligence, (AI), the rate and phases of change will be revolutionary in the coming years. Andrew McAfee and Erik Brynjolfsson from the MIT Initiative on the digital economy, rightly suggest that Existing business models rely on mind over machine, and product over technological platform. However, the new digital economy led by AI promises a reversal in such traditional business model. Mew Business models will be led by machines over minds and platforms over products.

Dr. Firend Alan Rasch, 2017

---

1.   *irend, Al. R. blog: http://drfirendblogs.blogspot.com/*

DEDICATION

This book is dedicated to the spirit of my father, who was a true professor, scholar, man of literature, an educator with love for laughter and life; who was such a compelling example for me.

This book is also dedicated for my beloved wife, for whom without her, I would not have been able to finish this book. I would also like to dedicate this book to my children, hoping to serve as an example of hard work and endurance. A special dedication to my students as well, with special appreciation for their assistance throughout the past four years.

Business Model Diagrams

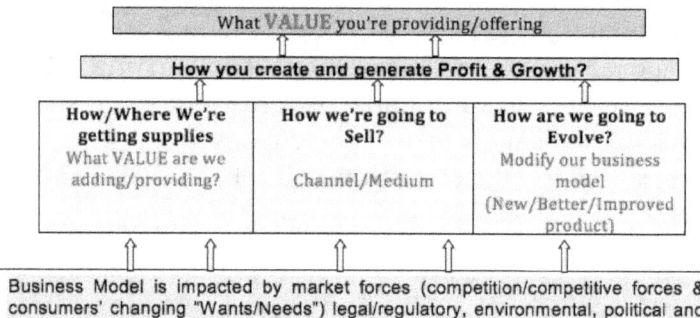

BUSINESS MODEL

It's the WAY a given business/organization is constructed. Business model is the architecture of organization' uniqueness which involves every element in the operation from the way you get your supplies to the way you sell your service/product. Business model is dynamic (evolving in nature) and not static. Static business models leads to an obsolete organizations.

What VALUE you're providing/offering

How you create and generate Profit & Growth?

How/Where We're getting supplies	How we're going to Sell?	How are we going to Evolve?
What VALUE are we adding/providing?	Channel/Medium	Modify our business model (New/Better/Improved product)

Business Model is impacted by market forces (competition/competitive forces & consumers' changing "Wants/Needs") legal/regulatory, environmental, political and technological forces. The **changing nature** of one or multiple element requires constant re-evaluation of the business model

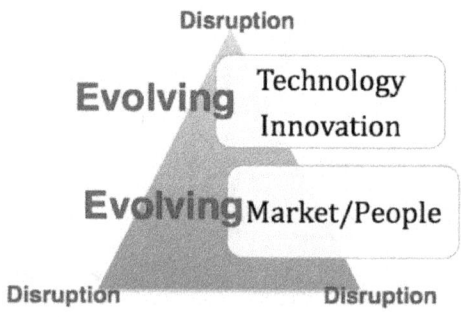

Disruption

Evolving Technology Innovation

Evolving Market/People

Disruption   Disruption

For Citation, please cite as following: *Firend, Al. R. 2017* drfirendblogs.blogspot.com

Legal Notes

GOOGLE INC.

Google

Company Background

Google Inc. is an American company that specializes in internet and cyber related services. It is the biggest search engine in the world. As at June 2014, Google owns approximately 68.75% of the worldwide search engine pie with Baidu coming in second place with 18.03% (Krawczyk, 2014). In 1998, Google was founded by two Ph.D. students named Sergey Brin and Larry Page at Stanford University. Google has then been growing ever since with 400 employees, formidable list of investors and about half-dozen of project managers (Carlson, 2014).

Problems and Solutions

Just like any company startups, Google's had no management layers between Page, the CEO and the engineers during the first year. However, as Google grew, more and more layers of management were added and Larry Page grew to hate it over the years. In July 2001, Larry Page decided to lay off all of his project managers as he suspected that the project managers were steering the engineers away from the projects he wanted them to work on (Carlson, 2014). There was one incident where Page had come up with a plan to make all the world's books searchable online but he found out that none of his engineers are working on it and he blamed the project managers for it.

Page then hired Wayne Rosing as the new VP of engineering where all engineers will report directly only to Rosing and Rosing will directly report to Page. Many thought Page was out of his mind including Stacey Sullivan who was Google's human resource manager, Bill Campbell who was Page's executive and Eric Schmidt who was Google's chairman as no one can self-organize and people need somewhere or someone to go to when they have problems (Carlson, 2014). Page ignored their advice and went on with his plan.

The plan did not stick for very long as problems and issues arose not long after. Resources were not allocated efficiently, effective or when people needed it (Carlson, 2014). Before long, it bred redundancy. Employees and engineers start to become demotivated as they do not

14

know where their work was headed and they wanted feedback very badly. To solve this issue, Google began hiring project managers once more and Schmidt was placed as Page and Brin's mentor and as the CEO of Google. Just as Apple Inc. kicked Steve Jobs out of the company, Google although, did not kick Page out, they forced him to hire a CEO that would supervise him and ignored his other wishes after that (Carlson, 2014). And just like Jobs, Page came back with new resolutions, attitude and ambitions that also contributed to Google's success today.

Business Model

Google provide its users with many valued services, which include their main and most popular web search that are used by many people around the globe. It was so successful that the phrase "Let's Google It" became widely used globally. Due to the fact that the majority of users are using their web search, their advertisement services using Adwords which is a self-service auction-based advertising program is also very popular (BMIMatters, 2012). Google has also extended their advertising program using Adsense where Google allows advertisers to reach out further to more users to the Google Network users' webpage. When a Google Network user shows the advertiser's ads in their

15

page, they also earn a small amount of portion from the revenue earned by Google.

Google also came up with DoubleClick technology so that users can advertise using videos, images, pictures, text and many other different interactive ads that will be published on Google Network users' webpage, Google Finance and also on Youtube (BMIMatters, 2012). Besides that, learning from Apple, Google came out with an OS called Android that is used on smart phones and a platform called Chrome OS. Android is used by Samsung, Acer, Asus, Oppo and many others while Chrome OS on the other hand is widely used by many as their web browser.

With the wide variety of services and values provided by Google, not all are free. Google's main revenue comes from its advertising services. Take "Adwords" for example. Adwords generates Google's revenue by Cost per Click or CPC where advertisers pay Google each time someone clicks on their ads. It seems that "Adsense" is the one generating the biggest portion of Google's revenue. In 2009, Google had generated approximately $21 billion in revenue and Adsense contributed 95% of it (Google and the Fundamentals of Internet Business, 2010). Although Google has evolved its services in terms of its web browsing, Google Search and creating operating systems, none of has yet shown results that could turn into Google's major revenue generator.

Google's costs lie in four major key areas. The first being the research and development are where Google consistently comes up with new ways to improve and evolve their current services and to create as well as innovate new ones. R&D usually requires very heavy investment and can be considered as a vital and a key activity of Google. Secondly, Google's costs lie in their data center operations. There are approximately 1 million servers in data centers globally that processes almost 1 billion searches every day and so Google has to invest heavily in this area to maintain, manage and upkeep the data center in order for them to not crash.

In addition to that, traffic acquisition is also one of Google's major costs where it consists of money being paid to Google Network webpages that is under the Adsense program and to partners who helped to distribute Google Toolbar and many other products or drive traffic to Google's webpages (Google and the Fundamentals of Internet Business, 2010). Lastly, like any other company Google's incur costs in their marketing and sales department in order to manage, maintaining the sales and support team worldwide. These costs go also to the promotional and advertising expenses.

The success of a business model lies also in its key activities. The first and foremost key activity of Google is their research and development. As technology these days are growing and evolving rapidly around the globe, Google has to constantly come up with new ideas, innovations and to also improve their current services or being risked taken out of the game with other big players. Secondly it is to maintain and manage their IT infrastructure. To accommodate the amount of servers and data they have in Google, Google has to consistently upgrade and maintain their IT infrastructure to accommodate the evolving of technology and to support new services.

Google's strategic partners help to increase and extend its reach to users that increase its effectiveness and efficiency. In 2013, Google announced its partnership with Facebook Inc. (Neal, 2013). Google's DoubleClick users can now purchase and put up their ads on Facebook that provides Google's users with more value and in turn generates more revenue for Facebook. Other Google's partners include Youtube, Twitter, Samsung, Microsoft and many others.

Google's clients are considered vital with the sustainability of Google in the ever-changing and competitive market. They usually comprise the average internet users that are all around the world, advertisers or advertising agencies that used Google's Adwords and Adsense services widely, Google Network Users that contributed to Google's revenue through Adsense and Mobile devices developer that uses Android like Samsung, Oppo, Xiaomii, Acer and Asus.

Employees are considered as an important asset of every company. Of course, this includes Google. In order to maintain, retain and to not stress out employees, Google provides them with various benefits due to their amazing work culture. Some of them are:

1. **Google provides its employees with special benefits;** For instance, in order to promote and inspire their employees to use greener and cleaner techs, Google once provided employees with $5000 so that they can purchase a hybrid car.

2. **Google provides a wide-range of gourmet meals set;** Employees in Google are provided gourmet meals 3 times a day and most of them claimed that the food serve is a lot better than food serve in a 5-star restaurant

3. **Google believes that employees should not have to go more than 150 feet just for food;** That is why Google provides food stations everywhere within 150 feet for employees to snack on whenever they feel like it.

4. **Google provides their employees with bicycles around Google campus;** This is to make sure that their employees do not need to walk through their humongous campuses and it is also to promote the usage of greener technologies.

5. **Google is a canine friendly organization;** As long as their furry pets are well-behaved, employees can bring them to the office with them.

(Reference: Adapted from Steegle, n.d.)

The Future

In the near future, Google can expect to face an intense competition from other major players such as Microsoft and Facebook. Microsoft has been gaining market share by introducing Windows 8, an OS targeting mobile devises to compete with Google's Android. This will mostly affect Google's revenue. In terms of Facebook, social media has been becoming more and more popular these days and this could threaten Google's dominance globally as Facebook has been evolving and increasing their features.

Additionally, no doubt Google has come up with many different products but many of them generate little profit and some services may be even free to use. For example, Google created Google Reader. When first launched, Google Reader was indeed popular but due to the recent rise in the social media, its popularity went down drastically. Additionally, iGoogle that allows users to streamline their usual inter-web activities soon proved to be irrelevant these days due to the rapid evolution of today's mobile and web applications. If Google continues to introduce new services like these, their revenue will most likely drop.

Conclusion

In conclusion, a company's business model plays an essential role in its effectiveness, efficiency and sustainability. Its employees, customers, partners and adaptability to face challenges also help it to grow. A very good culture on the other hand helps to elevate employee's stress, to promote CSR, forge ties, reduce fatigue, increases cooperation and teamwork between employees as well as retaining their loyalty and commitment to Google.

Google Alphabet Inc.

Alphabet is a conglomerate company that was founded in October 2nd 2015 by both founders of Google, Larry Page and Sergey Brin. Alphabet is currently serving as Google's parent company. The management in charge of Alphabet will be the same as the ones managing Google where Larry Page is the CEO, Sergey Brin as President, Eric Schmidt as the Executive Chairman, Ruth Porat as the CFO and David Drummond as the Chief Counsel (Rosoff, 2015). Google now has become the biggest subsidiary of Alphabet that will be overseeing Google's other ambitious projects such as Google X, Google Ventures, Google Optics, Calico and Nest Labs that were once under Google's research (Titcomb, 2015).

Business model

The main objective behind Alphabet's creation was investors demand of Google's diversification strategy, and whether or not their investments are paying off in the long run. Specially as google started to generate huge amounts of profits and sitting on cash that can be invested elsewhere. Over the years, Page and Brin have extensively diversified Google from its core purpose as an internet search engine. From email to maps and operating systems, Google has invested in home gadgets, high speed internets as well as driverless cars which are considered as something irrelevant to Google's core business, yet essential to the creation of parallel and new technologies. Due to the diversification of Google, analysts also found it hard to figure out how Google's core business is performing (Titcomb, 2015). With google busy making their core business (search engine) better and stronger, and acquiring new businesses overtime to capitalize on new technological opportunities and diversify their core capabilities, it was wise to split the the core business of Google, from the newly acquired businesses and investments.

The founders see the new structure as a win-win solution for them all. Both Page and Brian can now focus one the bigger picture while taking a step back from running Google everyday, while investors get a clearer picture of the company they invested in. Page's number two man Mr. Pichai, will run Google since he proved himself as effective manager (Titcomb, 2015). This remodeling of the business also shows that even though both Page and Brian are not holding majority ownership of Google because of the dual-class share structure, yet, they are still in control and able to provide the two entities to grow separately. This split will also allow both companies to draw from each other's strengths. So what will google core business be in a decade from now? May something completely different from search engines.

References

Osterwalder, A., & Pigneur, Y. (2010). *Business model generation: a handbook for visionaries, game changers, and challengers*. John Wiley & Sons.

Hedman, J., & Kalling, T. (2003). The business model concept: theoretical underpinnings and empirical illustrations. *European journal of information systems, 12*(1), 49-59.

Chesbrough, H., & Rosenbloom, R. S. (2002). The role of the business model in capturing value from innovation: evidence from Xerox Corporation's technology spin-off companies. *Industrial and corporate change, 11*(3), 529-555.

Morris, M., Schindehutte, M., & Allen, J. (2005). The entrepreneur's business model: toward a unified perspective. *Journal of business research, 58*(6), 726-735.

Wurster, T. S. (1999). *Blown to bits: How the new economics of information transforms strategy*. Harvard Business School Press.

Hofer, C. W. (1975). Toward a contingency theory of business strategy. *Academy of Management journal, 18*(4), 784-810.

Ghemawat, P. (2003). Semiglobalization and international business strategy. *Journal of International Business Studies, 34*(2), 138-152.

Joia, L. A. (2000). Measuring intangible corporate assets: linking business strategy with intellectual capital. *Journal of Intellectual capital, 1*(1), 68-84.

Cagliano, R., Caniato, F., & Spina, G. (2003). E-business strategy: how companies are shaping their supply chain through the internet. *International Journal of Operations & Production Management, 23*(10), 1142-1162.

Apple Inc.

Company Background

The Apple Inc. was co-founded by Steven Wozniak and marketed by Steve Jobs who were college dropouts in 1976. The two of them set up a garage in Jobs' family garage after selling a van for some extra start-up cash to build computers (Mittan, 2010). Apple Computer was officially incorporated on January 3, 1977 (Mittan, 2010). Steve made a deal Mike Markkula, an enthusiastic formal Intel executive who invested $250,000 in their business when he eventually sets out to find venture capitalists to fund Apple's expansion due to the breakthrough in Apple II. In 1977, Jobs and Markkula hired Michael Scott as Apple's first president and Chief Executive Officer (CEO) which confused many as to why Wozniak or Jobs were not chosen to hold that position (Clark, 2009).

Problems and Solutions

In 1985, there were conflicts within the management in Apple and there was increased in resentment against Jobs with his way of managing the team. In April 1985, there was a discussion of re-organizing the company structure by the board and everyone agreed that there should be a new manager for the Mac team, namely Apple France executive Jean-Louis Gassee (allabout Steve Jobs.com, n.d.). Jobs were still the chairman of the board from May – September 1985 must to everyone's amazement. But, he had a lot of time in his hands and he tried to find what would be his next step. Jobs then decided to leave Apple in September 1984 to create another company called NeXT (All about Steve Jobs.com, n.d.).

Throughout the next eleven years or so, Apple continued developing desktops and operating system but the company was not able to recover fully after Jobs left. John Sculley who was Apple's CEO from 1983, left the company in October 1993 due to the extreme pressure to increase Apple's sale and market share with new services and products (Mittan, 2010). Michael Spindler who was the President of Apple Europe was promoted as the new CEO who resigned three years later. After that Apple promoted Gil Amelio who was one of the board members in 1996 and then removed him from that position in late 1996 as Apple's stock prices continue to decline. Knowing that he was the best choice, Apple re-hired Jobs as the company's new CEO. With his strong leadership style and innovative vision, Jobs finally made a triumphant return and introduced the products like the iMac, Power Mac G4, Power Mac G4 Cube, Mac OS X and the iPod. Jobs finally introduced the iPhone and its revolutionary touch-screen interface in his most memorable keynote presentation ever

Subsequently, the MacBook, MacBook Air, the iPad, iPhone 3G, iPhone 3GS, iPhone 4 and the iCloud was introduced in the later years. After Job's long battle with pancreatic cancer, he resigned as CEO in August 2011 and Tim Cook took his place as CEO of Apple. Following Job's demise in October 2011, Apple purchased C3 Technologies and acquired Anobit. Apple continues to grow till this very by remaining as the leading smartphone manufacturer in the U.S. for the three-month period ending in June (Bora, 2014).

Business Model

Apple offers its customers a variety of product. Apple's first product was the Apple I, It was then followed by Apple II and Apple Lisa. The Macintosh was later introduced as Apple's original and iconic computer. It was build to target mainly at the education, creative, professional and home markets. Since it was introduced, the Macintosh has seen quite a number of evolutions.

Apple continues to further innovate and develop their products in the market. It came out with the iPod in 2001, iPhone in 2007, iPad in 2010 and MacBook in 2006. The iPod is a revolutionizing portable music device that allows thousands of songs at the user's disposal in one sleek product. iPhone is a smartphone that can contain many different apps that assist the user in their daily life. It is like computer that is packed up in one small device. The iPad on the other hand, marked Apple's return to tablet computers that was considerably more successful than previous efforts (*The Telegraph n.d.*). As for the MacBook, Apple's laptops have become the weapon of choice of many worlds' design professionals from the Macintosh Portable to the Macbook.

Apple has also been developing their Mac Operating System to cope up with the technological change. This can be seen in the table below.

Date	Operating System

8th Jun, 1978	Apple Dos
24th Jan, 1984	System 1
25th Apr, 1985	System 2
25th Jan, 1986	System 3
7th Jan, 1987	System 4
5th Apr, 1988	System 6
13th May, 1991	System 7
26th Jul, 1997	Mac OS 8
23rd Oct, 1999	Mac OS 9
24th Mar, 2001	Cheetah
25th Sep, 2001	Puma
23rd Aug, 2002	Jaguar
24th Oct, 2003	Panther
29th Apr, 2005	Tiger
26th Oct, 2007	Leopard
8th Jun, 2009	Snow Leopard
20th Jul, 2011	Mac OS Lion
25th July, 2012	Mountain Lion
22nd Oct, 2013	Mavericks
16th Oct, 2014	Yosemite
30th Sept, 2015	El Capitan

Source: Adapted from Shadyramadan, n.d.

Besides that, in terms of promotion, Apple did not really advertise their products if anyone noticed (McCormac, 2013). Their advertising budget is considered to be the lowest compared to both Samsung and Microsoft. From the table below, it can be seen that Apple's advertising budget is most definitely not the largest if compared to its rivals' budget, but it is absolutely the one that is used the most successfully.

Company	2010	2011	2012
Apple Inc.	$691 million	$933 million	$1 billion
Samsung Electronics Co., Ltd.	$2.75 billion	$2.63 billion	$4.3 billion
Microsoft Corporation	$1.6 billion	$1.9 billion	$1.6 billion

Source: Adapted from Strategic Management Insight, 2014

What people had been seeing are some other companies advertising for Apple. Apple iPhone ads are actually paid by mobile phone operators who want to advertise the fact that they are selling the iPhones. When these mobile operators want to tell the whole world that they are selling the iPhones, they do not only pay the bills, however, Apple imposed a strict requirement on how the adverts must look and the information that it contains (McCormac, 2013). This is partly why Apple's entire adverts for products looked the same.

Apple has also provided customers with values when it positions itself to be a pioneer of producing high tech and innovative products in the mobile (iPhone), computer (Macintosh, MacBook) and electronics (iPod, iPad) industry as well as the quality that comes with it. It is one of the original hardware producers in the market that have control over the manufacturing of their products and they also create their own internal components for the core of its computers (Maha, 2012). Apple has also done some of the best innovation under the iPhone's airbrushed hood (Time, 2014). While consumers see the iPhones having the same shape and size over and over again, they assumed nothing has changed. In reality, Apple's biggest accomplishment is maintaining its compact design while keeping up with Samsung's powerful shape-shifting phones.

Apple expanded its consumer reach by building many new retail outlets, owing and operating around the world in the last ten years. It has also placed their products from iPods, iPads, and iPhones in about every store that sells electronics these days. Also, from numerous retail outlets to a great e-commerce website, like Amazon, Apple's website, making their products to be easily accessible to purchase.

In terms of strategic partners, Apple does not seem to need any. With the $40 billion in cash that Apple has reserved they have the potential to buy up companies with patents that would allow Apple to grow past the limit that their current patents restrain them to (Cranford, 2013). The popular apps that Apple turned into or enhancing their own by acquiring other companies are Siri (Siri Inc and Navauris), iTunes (Concept.io and Beats Music & Beats Electronics), Maps (Spotsetter, BroadMap, Embark Inc, Hopstop.com Inc, Locationary, Poly 9 and Placebase), Apple TV (Matcha.tv), iBooks (BookLamp) and many more (AAPL Investors.net, 2014).

Apple's revenue also comes mainly from the sale of only both iPad and iPhone. For years the iPhone and iPad has been the main profit driver for Apple even though it offers a variety of products (CBC News, 2014). Apple can thank sales in China for the important boost. More than half of the company's revenue comes from the iPhone, which also offers the bulk of profits. This actually makes Apple dangerously dependent on a single product that it apparently can't charge as much for.

The Future

As always, Apple will continue developing their iPhones, iPads, Macs, Operating Systems and Apps in the future by adding in more functions and features in a simple manner. Besides that, due to the fact that Apple's App Store had encountered and suffered one of its first breach when it was hacked, Apple has decided to make it possible for the Chinese to download its features and tools for building many more apps on their own. Apple was told by the Chinese app developers that they have resorted in downloading the hacked software kits from third party and unauthorized sources because of the slow speed they encounter while downloading from Apple's official servers.

Conclusion

In conclusion, Apple's business model has proven to be effective for its growth and development. Its quality and continuous innovations will continue to place it as one of the toughest competitor to beat in the technology industry. Being able to tackle and solve challenges also comes from its effectiveness and efficiency in their leading and managing.

References

Grant, R. M. (2016). *Contemporary strategy analysis: Text and cases edition.* John Wiley & Sons.

Teece, D. J. (2010). Business models, business strategy and innovation. *Long range planning, 43*(2-3), 172-194.

Bharadwaj, A., El Sawy, O., Pavlou, P., & Venkatraman, N. (2013). Digital business strategy: toward a next generation of insights.

Amit, R., & Zott, C. (2012). Creating value through business model innovation. *MIT Sloan Management Review, 53*(3), 41.

Tallon, P. P. (2007). A process-oriented perspective on the alignment of information technology and business strategy. *Journal of Management Information Systems, 24*(3), 227-268.

Wheelen, T. L., Hunger, J. D., Hoffman, A. N., & Bamford, C. E. (2017). *Strategic management and business policy.* pearson.

Spender, J. C. (2014). *Business strategy: Managing uncertainty, opportunity, and enterprise.* OUP Oxford.

Ghezzi, A., Cortimiglia, M. N., & Frank, A. G. (2015). Strategy and business model design in dynamic telecommunications industries: A study on Italian mobile network operators. *Technological Forecasting and Social Change, 90,* 346-354.

Halal, W. E. (2015). Business strategy for the technology revolution: competing at the edge of creative destruction. *Journal of the Knowledge Economy, 6*(1), 31-47.

Rothaermel, F. T. (2015). *Strategic management.* McGraw-Hill Education.

LOTTE

Company Background

Lotte confectionary is a South Korean company headquartered in Seoul under the Lotte Group of companies. The company was established in 1967, to date it covers a wide range of snacks including gum, candies, cookies and chocolates. Some of the famous products from Lotte include Crunky candy bar, Chi-Choc cookie, Peppero and Koala's March. In 2008, Lotte took over Guylian, a Belgium company that makes specialty chocolates. Lotte is currently the third largest chewing gum manufacturer in the world with The Juicy Fresh, Spearmint and Freshmint as old-time favorites for more than four decades while the Xylitol range is currently being the favorite in the market.

Business Model

The Xylitol range is unique because it uses Finnish Xylitol made from birch trees and the content of the natural sweetener is more than 50% which beats all the other gums in the market that uses artificial sweeteners. Xylitol is also known to help prevent cavities.

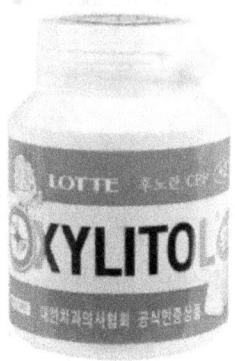

Xylitol chewing gum by Lotte

The battle for succession

Currently, Lotte is surrounded by the family scandal involving father and sons of the family-owned conglomerate. The 92 year old founder of Lotte, Mr Shin Kyuk Ho, is the father of two sons – Shin Dong Joo and Shin Dong Bin. Both of his sons are intensely battling to be the successor of the controlling seat, anticipating the death of their father soon. In the feud, his younger son, Shin Dong Bin has ousted his father as the General Chairman of Lotte Hotel and Lotte Group.

Family feud: Key players in succession battle

A look at who's who in the Shin family which controls Lotte Group, one of South Korea's largest business conglomerates.

Shin Kyuk Ho, 92
• Founder and general chairman of Lotte Group. Caught in an ongoing succession battle between his two sons. Born in Ulsan but left to study in Japan in 1942. Started Lotte Confectionery in 1948.

Shin Young Ja, 73
• Elder daughter of Mr Shin and his first wife, who died in 1951. Chairman of Lotte Welfare Foundation. She is siding with the elder son.

Shin Dong Joo, 61
• Elder son of Mr Shin from his second marriage to Ms Hatsuko Shigemitsu. Former vice-chairman of Japan-based Lotte Holdings, ousted in January. Ranked 22nd richest man in South Korea this year by Forbes magazine, with a net worth of US$1.5 billion.

Shin Dong Bin, 60
• Second son. Chairman of Lotte Group and current head of Lotte Holdings. Ranked 19th richest man in South Korea this year by Forbes with a net worth of US$1.7 billion.

A hierarchy drawn by Straits Times illustrating the family feud.

The right marketing

In a statement made by Shin Dong Bin, he apologized for the scandal and vowed an all-out effort to normalize situation and will have a meeting with his father. These types of scandals are frown upon in Asian countries, which are know to value the elderly and put utmost importance in respect. Several media outlets in Korea has lambasted Shin Dong Bin for his actions especially since Mr Shin Kyuk Ho himself once said that, "A company should bot be shaken by family feud".

Shin Dong Joo, who was in charge of Lotte confectionary was originally considered to be the heir due to his seniority but his younger brother proved to be a strong contender with his aggressive operations and international's expansion.

Observers have given warnings to Lotte that a very public family fight will tarnish the image of the company. The controversy has also weighed on Lotte's share prices. The week the news broke, Lotte's stock prices sank over 8% and it indicates stockholder's fear over the pitfall of the company.

Experts are saying that at times like this, transparent rules and procedures are paramount as succession battles usually end badly in the public eye. Numerous reports surrounding the battle will only bring the company's image down and without proper damage control, the reputation of the company will plummet.

References

http://seekingalpha.com/article/3687806-the-economic-flaw-in-alibabas-most-damaging-headline-risk-counterfeits

http://www.nytimes.com/2015/05/19/business/international/kering-sues-alibaba-again-over-counterfeit-luxury-goods.html?_r=0

http://money.cnn.com/2015/05/17/investing/alibaba-lawsuit-fakes/

http://www.financialmagazin.com/alibaba-group-holding-limited-nysebaba-sellers-increased-by-6-5-their-shorts/

http://www.bloomberg.com/news/articles/2015-08-14/kering-s-gucci-wins-order-barring-alibaba-merchants-fake-goods

http://www.cosmeticsandtoiletries.com/regulatory/region/asia/3941496.html

http://www.chinadaily.com.cn/china/2006-10/25/content_716106.htm

http://www.zalora.com.my/Age-Protect-Set-352627.html

http://www.ft.com/intl/cms/s/0/31a5f0ce-635b-11db-bc82-0000779e2340.html#axzz3tsKri1l9

http://discoversk-ii.wix.com/home#!brand-history/c1a0l

https://www.gsb.stanford.edu/faculty-research/case-studies/sk-ii-china-managing-public-relations

http://www.bjreview.com.cn/business/txt/2006-12/20/content_51357.htm

https://en.wikipedia.org/wiki/Samsung_Electronics

http://www.cnet.com/news/samsung-continues-to-rule-over-apple-in-smartphone-market/

https://en.wikipedia.org/wiki/Apple_Inc._v._Samsung_Electronics_Co.

http://www.snopes.com/politics/satire/samsung.asp

http://www.nytimes.com/2012/08/25/technology/jury-reaches-decision-in-apple-samsung-patent-trial.html?_r=0

http://www.huffingtonpost.com/2012/08/24/apple-samsung-lawsuit-verdict_n_1829268.html

http://www.reuters.com/article/us-samsung-shares-idUSBRE87Q00120120827#bzB2zDxj6fE9uv5c.97

http://www.knowyourmobile.com/samsung/samsung-galaxy-note-5/23385/samsung-galaxy-note-5-vs-samsung-galaxy-note-4-phablet-kings

https://www.google.com/finance?q=KRX:005930

http://www.cityam.com/230330/why-strong-brands-are-stock-market-darlings

http://www.themalaysianinsider.com/malaysia/article/salang-astro-broadcasting-disruption-during-rain-cannot-be-eliminated-completely

https://www.malaysiakini.com/letters/167483

http://www.astro.com.my/mediaroom/articles/art_astro-ASTRO-DELIVERS-DOUBLE-DIGIT-GROWTH-IN-FY14.html

http://www.japantimes.co.jp/news/2015/12/09/business/corporate-business/south-korean-japanese-snack-maker-lotte-go-public-next-year/#.VmjvdukxHZs

http://www.lotteconf.co.kr/eng/info/info_view.asp?mn=030300&iBoard=30&BD_IDX=33

https://en.wikipedia.org/wiki/Lotte_Confectionery

http://www.straitstimes.com/asia/east-asia/son-boots-out-father-in-battle-for-south-korean-giant-lotte

http://www.straitstimes.com/asia/east-asia/son-boots-out-father-in-battle-for-south-korean-giant-lotte

AMAZON

amazon

Company Background

In 1994, Jeff Bezos founded Amazon in his garage in Bellevue, Washington. Initially, the company was incorporated as "Cadabra" and a year later renamed to Amazon after a lawyer misheard it as "cadaver". The founder chose "Amazon" after looking through the dictionary because it was the biggest river in the world, different and exotic just as he planned for his store to be and has visions to make his store the biggest in the world. In 1995, the company went public and took its business online as Amazon.com.

The company began its business as an online bookstore and later expanded in the late 1990s to offer a wide selection of books, CDs, DVDs, electronics, toys, tools, home furnishings and housewares and apparel. Amazon.com also sells products from well-known retailers including TOYS R US, Target, Borders and Expedia among others through third-party agreements. Amazon.com is considered a pioneer and first to market the idea of online retailing concept. Today, Amazon is one of the most innovative of online retailers, and has experienced both success and failure in its business model.

Business Model/Strategy

Amazon has based its business model on a multi-level e-commerce strategy. The company started off in the early days on a Business-to-Consumer relationships and Business-to-Business relationships model. Then, the company realized the value and importance of customer reviews as part of the product descriptions and moved to incorporate Customer-to-Business transactions into its business model as well. Almost anyone can sell almost anything using its platform. In addition, there is now a new program, which let affiliates build entire websites on Amazon's platform.

Amazon kick-start their initial business plans in a very unusual way. It did not project to make a profit for up to five years of operations. This has concerned the stockholders if the company is able to make profit fast enough to justify their investments, or to even survive in the long-term. At the start of the 21st century, when the dot-com bubble burst and along the way destroying many e-companies, somehow, Amazon has managed to survived, and achieve growth to become a huge player in online sales. In the fourth quarter of 2001, Amazon reported its first profit of $5 million and revenues of more than $1 billion With this success it has proven that Amazon's unconventional business model works and could succeed over time. Amazon has three lines of businesses: product and service sales, publishing, and digital content.

Amazon Retail

The company started off as an online bookseller and later on expands into music, movies, and then into electronics and household goods. The online retail line includes products by Amazon and other large online sellers who use Amazon to sell their products in addition to selling them through their own websites. Amazon also leases space for these retailers and processed the sales while the retailer does order fulfilment.

Another part of its retail strategy is to serve as a channel for retailers to sell their products and taking a commission of every purchase. Amazon doesn't stock everything that is

43

sold through its website therefore it does not have to maintain inventory on slower-selling products. This strategy has enable Amazon to expand its available selection without increasing in overhead costs.

Amazon built an online retail business with three objectives:

1. Best prices: Amazon products are generally offered at a discount.

2. A wide selection: Amazon has the largest selection of goods in a particular category.

3. Convenience: Amazon focuses on the customer and try making each purchase as an enjoyable experience, easy-to-use customer interface and reliable delivery from fully automated warehouses. Amazon also offers a no-nonsense returns policy.

Amazon Marketplace

To extend their retail model further, Amazon introduced a third-party selling platform called Marketplace for sale of new and used products by small sellers to compete with eBay. Similar with Amazon Retail concept, this platform provides another revenue stream for the company without the need to stock products in its warehouses. Amazon provides the seller a platform and charges a commission based on a certain formula involving the selling price of the item while sellers handle advertising and shipping.

Amazon Web Services

Amazon's Internet services are not standalone line of business because it is connected with both its retail business and the Kindle ecosystem. Amazon has leveraged on this technology it developed by offering an increasing number of web services. Throughout the years, the business has expanded into manufacturing and distributing Kindle tablets. It was originally designed as an electronic book reader; today, the Kindle has become a fully functional device. However, the devices are sold at a loss and Amazon is hoping that customers will purchase enough electronic books and games to cover the loss.

Amazon also provides other Internet services known as Amazon Web Services (AWS) that was developed as a side business. With AWS, Amazon lease out its own server space to other companies and individuals.

Challenges and Solutions

Although Amazon has dominated online retail with a traditional retail business model; it does not come without challenges and issues to overcome. Over the years,

Amazon has been slapped with a few lawsuits. On May 12,1997, Amazon was sued by Barnes & Noble under allegation that Amazon's claim to be "the world's largest bookstore" was false and that Amazon is merely a book broker and not a bookstore. Later on, the suit was settled out of court and Amazon continued with same claim. On October 16, 1998 Walmart sued Amazon alleging that it had stolen trade secrets by hiring former Walmart executives. Again this suit was also settled out of court. However, Amazon had to reassign the former Walmart executives and implement internal restrictions.

Recently, Wal-Mart has expanded into the online space by acquiring online search technologies i.e. Torbit, a cloud-based website accelerator service; Inkiru, a predictive intelligence platform, Tasty Labs and also started building warehouses. Therefore, in a counteract effort and to compete with this, the company is planning to open its first store in Manhattan, which is a big shift from Amazon.com's business model at the same time, the company has not forgotten its roots and has been expanding its subscription customer base by keeping the product and services prices low.

Future

Amazon has managed to keep some things consistent over the years despite its diversified business lines. Regardless of products or services offered, their value proposition of price and convenience remains in all of its categories. These characteristics have allowed the company it to expand into new markets and strengthen relationship with customers.

One of the most recent ventures is Amazon Publishing, a tool for on demand publishing and giving new authors access to Amazon store. Amazon also recently launched AutoRip, a platform where music purchases from the past is automatically made available digitally and stored in a cloud database. This service is to be expanded to movies and books in the nearest future.

Amazon is also planning to venture into the same day delivery segment in some parts of the U.S. This segment has been proven to a big challenge to many providers of e-commerce. Many have tried and failed. [4] This venture would likely give Amazon the advantage to conquer another category that has yet to take off online: the grocery business. However, as a start it is likely that the service will only be limited to areas in closest proximity to its warehouses.

Amazon has applied e-commerce innovation to a variety of traditional business models. It is seen that Amazon will continue to dominate the online retail business as it continues to expand and explore new categories into the future. To thrive and be successful in the digital era, it is very important to execute business model well than to invent new business models from scratch as seen in Amazon's case.

References

Akter, S., Wamba, S. F., Gunasekaran, A., Dubey, R., & Childe, S. J. (2016). How to improve firm performance using big data analytics capability and business strategy alignment?. *International Journal of Production Economics*, *182*, 113-131.

Ritala, P., Golnam, A., & Wegmann, A. (2014). Coopetition-based business models: The case of Amazon. com. *Industrial Marketing Management*, *43*(2), 236-249.

Grant, R. M. (2016). *Contemporary strategy analysis: Text and cases edition.* John Wiley & Sons.

Pisano, G. P. (2015). You need an innovation strategy. *Harvard Business Review*, *93*(6), 44-54.

Aversa, P., Haefliger, S., Rossi, A., & Baden-Fuller, C. (2015). From business model to business modelling: Modularity and manipulation. In *Business models and modelling* (pp. 151-185). Emerald Group Publishing Limited.

Spender, J. C. (2014). *Business strategy: Managing uncertainty, opportunity, and enterprise*. OUP Oxford.

Wieland, H., Hartmann, N. N., & Vargo, S. L. (2017). Business models as service strategy. *Journal of the Academy of Marketing Science*, *45*(6), 925-943.

Gambles, I. (2017). *Making the business case: Proposals that succeed for projects that work*. Routledge.

Madsen, T. L., & Walker, G. (2015). *Modern competitive strategy*. McGraw Hill.

HUAWEI

HUAWEI

Company Background

Huawei of China is a leader in ICT solutions, supplying products and services to telecom carriers, consumers and businesses in over 170 regions and countries. It ranked 228 in the Global Fortune 500 revenue rankings of 2014, due to its revenue reaching around $46.5 billion. One of the strengths of Huawei is that they invest more than 10% of their annual sales revenue to Research & Development (R&D).

Furthermore, over 170,000 or 45% of Huawei employees are engaged in R&D. Another brand promise of Huawei is driving low-carbon economic growth, achieved through assisting industries and customers in improving their efficiency. This makes them an advocate of socioeconomic sustainability, providing secure and stable network

50

connections. Their aim is to build connect everyone and everything in an efficient system to spark infinite possibilities.

Huawei has a wide range of products and services available for different kinds of consumer and businesses[4]. Let us begin with consumers first, as that is what most people are familiar with. For the consumer market, they offer products in categories like mobile phones, tablets, and wearable devices, mobile broadband and smart homes. For businesses they offer products for telecom wireless networks, fixed networks, core network, carrier software, network energy, IT, enterprise wireless, networks and Unified Communications and Collaboration (UC&C).

For services, they offer a variety of solutions for network carriers like consulting, customer experience management, system integration, managed services, customer support, network rollout and learning services. For enterprise services, they offer data centre planning & design, implementation, agile network planning & design, data migration, railway communication design & implementation, safe city design & implementation and finally technical & specialized support. All these vast array of services actually sheds light that Huawei is more than just a smart phone maker, it is on the way to becoming an IT giant to rival the rest of the market leaders.

Business Model

Looking into the 2014 annual report, their carrier business is their main source of revenue totaling 66.6% (192 CNY million), followed by their consumer business totaling 26% (75 CNY million) of revenue, 6.7% (19 CNY million) for Enterprise and 0.57% (1.6 CNY million) for Others. As for from which region the cash flows, first place is China at 37.7% (108 CNY million) of revenue, followed by the EMEA region (Europe, Middle East & Africa) at 35% (100 CNY million), then followed by Asia Pacific at 14.7% (42 CNY million), the Americas at 10.7% (30 CNY million) and the rest of the world at 1.75% (5 CNY million).

Their carrier business involves developing and manufacturing a variety of wireless networks, carrier software, fixed networks, core networks and serviced solutions to telecommunication providers. This is the bulk of the company's income, by being the infrastructure and backbone of communications. It is from this backbone that other businesses thrive and prosper, making Huawei an important part of modern business and communication.

Besides being in the carrier business, one of the more prevalent and visible part of Huawei's business segments is its phone business. This is especially true where most of the ads showing in Malaysia focus on its mobile phones more than its carrier business. This is most probably due to competition of already established carriers in Malaysia, such as Celcom, Digi and Maxis. Huawei's phone offerings are divided into different series which are the Mate series, P series, G series and the Nexus series. Its current flagship models are the Huawei Mate 8 and Mate S.

The Mate S emphasizes on touch, and its promotional video delivers impactful messages of how touch is an important language in life when it comes to connecting with other in our daily life. The video links that very important language in our hearts to the capability of the phone, which is what they call Interactive Touch. A function called Fingerprint 2.0 adds another sensor behind the phone where you can use your index finger for various functions, adding more depth to the touch dimensions of a smartphone.

Knuckle 2.0 is a fancy feature where your knuckle activates certain functions of the phone, again adding another dimension to the touch inputs a phone can detect. Special versions of the phone have pressure sensitive screen, further expanding the possible features that can be utilized. It can even be used to weight objects, showing the accuracy of its sensors. The Mate S is truly an advanced and fancy touch phone, which might clear the path to new trends and standards in the smartphone industry.

Challenges

The founder of Huawei, Ren Zhengfei was an officer in the Chinese army[3]. Due to this fact, some countries like the US have suspicions over Huawei's connection with the Chinese Government. Some suggested that the company went public to increase transparency. To solve this issue, he officially made a statement that going public would not be beneficial for the company, and for the first time very he had an interview with the western media.

The interview painted an image for him, of a Chinese non-combatant officer that was let go and he had to make a living. He also claimed to be a very shy person, with a very unpleasant personal life up to the point that his hobbies were only working and making money. Furthermore, he commented that his only regret was his inability to fulfill his obligations to his parents. This interview somewhat helps other people relate to him, because before this his personal profile has been much of a mystery. Whether this will stop the US from monitoring the company is unknown, but other countries like the UK are open to Huawei for business and in there lies better opportunity[3]. Also, the company has been publishing financial reports, available to anyone interested up to 2006 in their corporate website.

The Future

The future is in Virtual Reality (VR) and Augmented Reality (AR)[8]. Various corporations are engaging research institutions on the possibility and power of AR. Huawei Media Labs is the R&D division of Huawei, employing over 70,000 researchers in 16 centers. These centers are spread out in locations like Sweden, Germany, France, US, Russia, Italy, China and India. Furthermore, this group of researchers count for more than 45% of Huawei's total global workforce. This further emphasizes the importance of R&D in maintaining a market leader position in this competitive landscape.

In conclusion, Huawei is yet another rising company in the tech industry hailing from China. With the number of tech companies strongly emerging out of China, it is obvious why China is a powerhouse to be reckoned with. The trend of influential companies originating from China is becoming more and more apparent; therefore they need to remain innovative to stay ahead of the competition.

References

Fu, X., Sun, Z., & Ghauri, P. N. (2018). Reverse knowledge acquisition in emerging market MNEs: The experiences of Huawei and ZTE. *Journal of Business Research*.

Yan, J., Wang, L., & Xiong, J. (2017). Alcatel-Lucent falls, Huawei ascends: New product development makes the difference. *Journal of Business Strategy, 38*(1), 22-30.

De Cremer, D., & Tian, T. (2017). Is Compassionate Leadership a Driver of Huawei's Business Success?. *The European Business Review*.

Mao, H., & Zhang, X. (2016). The International Business Strategy of Chinese MNCs: How Chinese large private MNCs develop their international business strategy to achieve competitive advantages in culturally different markets.

Lee, H. O., & Shin, H. D. (2018). 2 Corporate strategy and the competitiveness of Korean electronics firms versus their Japanese and Chinese counterparts. *Strategic, Policy and Social Innovation for a Post-Industrial Korea: Beyond the Miracle*.

Micheli, J., & Carrillo, J. (2016). The Globalization Strategy of a Chinese Multinational: Huawei in Mexico. *Frontera Norte, 28*(56).

De Cremer, D. (2017). Making customer centricity work for your company. *The European Financial Review*, 64-67.

Suryadevara, N. K., & Mukhopadhyay, S. C. (2018). Internet of Things: A Review and Future Perspective. *Reliance*.

Vlachos, I. P. (2016). Reverse logistics capabilities and firm performance: The mediating role of business strategy. *International Journal of Logistics Research and Applications*, *19*(5), 424-442.

Nardon, L., Steers, R. M., & Sanchez-Runde, C. J. (2018). Developing multicultural competence. *Reliance*.

Motohashi, K. (2015). *Global business strategy: Multinational corporations venturing into emerging Markets*. Springer Open.

Wright, T., & Snook, C. J. (2016). *Digital Sense: The Common Sense Approach to Effectively Blending Social Business Strategy, Marketing Technology, and Customer Experience*. John Wiley & Sons.

Esposito, M., Tse, T., & Xiong, L. (2017). Business as Usual?. *European Business Review*.

Joo, S. H., Oh, C., & Lee, K. (2016). Catch-up strategy of an emerging firm in an emerging country: analysing the case of Huawei vs. Ericsson with patent data. *International Journal of Technology Management*, *72*(1-3), 19-42.

Roll, M. (2015). Branding—The Driver of a Successful Business Strategy. In *Asian Brand Strategy (Revised and Updated)* (pp. 15-36). Palgrave Macmillan, London.

Lee, S. H., Kwon, Y., Lee, J. H., & Park, Y. I. (2016). Creative Imitation as Catch-up Strategy: A Business Model. *Asian Journal of Innovation & Policy*, *5*(1).

Viaene, S. (2017). How To Catch A Moving Target in the Digital World. *The European Business Review*, *8*(6), 29-34.

Xia, W., & Gan, D. Z. (2017). The Marketing strategy of HUAWEI Smartphone in China.

Zhu, H., Zhang, M. Y., & Lin, W. (2017). The fit between business model innovation and demand-side dynamics: catch-up of China's latecomer mobile handset manufacturers. *Innovation*, *19*(2), 146-166.

CADBURY INDIA LTD.

Cadbury

Company Background

Cadbury (India) is a private limited business, established in 1948. The manufacturing facilities have been gradually set up. Cadbury (India) has 71% of market share while Nestle owns 20%; Ferrero has 6% and others 3% in India. Cadbury has been able to keep "Cadbury means quality" and achieve its objective "Cadbury is in every pocket" consistently. The strategies implementation and execution of Cadbury to achieve its ultimate goals by proactive means of organizational development and product innovation will mainly be discussed in this article.

Cadbury strikes to achieve its marketing objectives, financial objectives and overall objectives via "5 Generic Strategies", mainly "Best Cost Provider" strategy and sustain as market leader in chocolate confessionary industry in India. Cadbury set a transparent target of both narrow buyer and broad buyer, generate the strategies to anticipate the demands and supply needs of the market, and execute them by using standard "Balance Scorecard" for chocolate industry to measure and continuously improve total quality management (TQM) at operational level, functional level and business level. According to Cadbury world marketing team (2009), the strategies used by Cadbury to sustain its competitive advantages in the market over the rival are as follows.

Cadbury (India) targets everyone within the age of 5 to 60 years all over India. It focuses on both genders throughout the life cycle (young, single, married and elder) regardless of the income and educational level (from primary and university). Cadbury creates and sustains its competitive advantages over the rival by portraying its products in different perspectives, but not just another chocolate in the market. Cadbury positions its brand image properly by connection with people emotion. At the same time, Cadbury continues to improve the quality of existing products and create new products.

Cadbury changes the attitude of customer towards its products. It creates the image that it is more special if people celebrate their wedding, marriage anniversary or Valentine's Day with Cadbury chocolate. It also produces products to be given as gifts with both beautiful and adorable designs not only as birthday presents but also as graduating presents for young children, teenagers and young adults. Moreover, it tries to generate the value as necessary value to have tried Cadbury to be up to date. As Cadbury is a world recognized brand, the value is able to be created as necessary value and it becomes the culture in India to try the Cadbury.

Cadbury continuously strikes for total quality management (TQM) of its products via product research and development (R&D). Packaging is one of the best examples of Cadbury striking to meet the demand and need of customer. As shown in Figure 1.1, the packaging had been changed from one design to another in response to meet the demand of the customer. The brighter color was chosen in designing the package to easily visible for customer their favorite bar on the shelf. The reclose packaging feature was also used as customer prefers resalable packaging. Cadbury won gold award at "Global Design Pent awards" in 2013 for its thoughtful and amazing packaging design. Cadbury uses SIX SIGMA method for market research and found out that customers are becoming more aware of health issues and conscious about the food and calories they consume. Therefore, Cadbury also includes the nutritional factors on the package (Casey, 2014). Not only calories for the whole bar but also calories per portion are also printed on the front of the pack, but sugar and fat content appears on the back as shown in Figure 1.

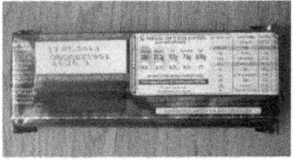

Figure 1: Cadbury's Packaging Evaluation   *Figure 1.2:* Nutritional Factor on Pack

As Cadbury is world-recognized product, it has the competitive advantage for its quality. People trust the brand and believe that it is a fine quality branded product. But

Cadbury does not stop trying to innovative and create new tastes for the customer. Cadbury produces its products in bar, block, roll, candy and boxes designs. The products are also designed for special yearly occasion such as Easter, Christmas and Halloween. A variety of choices are provided for each design.

Through market research, Cadbury found out that the customer experience different tastes according to the shape of the chocolate. Therefore, Cadbury changes the design of chocolate block from rigid block to round shape. Therefore, we can see that Cadbury always strikes to provide gourmet quality chocolate to customer and to meet the demand of the products in the market.

As Cadbury target audience is very large as mentioned above, Cadbury produces it products, which can be affordable to different level of incomes. It differentiates the products based on the weight and price. However, Cadbury makes the different tastes available for all different size to provide variety of choices for all customers.

Cadbury distributes its products to all areas in India via manufactures to whole seller, whole seller to retailers, retailers to customer in both urban and rural areas.

Cadbury products are available at all different convenient shops in response to the lifestyle changes of customer. Customer usually buys snacks including chocolate at convenient shop rather than going to shopping mall and buys it. However, for some of Cadbury products with high price are more available on urban areas. In this way, Cadbury ensures its marketing objective "Cadbury in every pocket" and financial objects to be profitable.

Cadbury communicates with its target market in valued added strategy. It focuses on image of its products, performance and value of its products, and connects it with people emotion. Cadbury also use aggressive advertisement campaign and billboard advertisement to reach out to its audience. Amitabh Bacchanal, one of the world popular actors, is hired as its brand ambassador to for media communication.

In term of crisis management, Cadbury India Ltd faced the crisis of "live worms occurred in Dairy Milk chocolate bars". Cadbury took an immediate and fast action to minimize the damage and call back all the batches of chocolate bar during the same time line. Cadbury India Ltd. has begun investigations into reports that live worms were found in its Dairy Milk chocolate bars, the company said in a statement. "We are concerned about these reports and are investigating it," a company spokesperson said. The Maharashtra Food and Drugs Administration (FDA) had announced Monday that it would prosecute Cadbury India Ltd. after tests indicated "insect infestations" in the chocolate samples tested.

FDA officials conducted raids at the *Talegaon* plant of the company as well at sockets' premises throughout Maharashtra. The authorities have, however, decided not to shut down the plant or cancel the company's license to manufacture chocolates. *"The chocolates have been out for sale since July 2003 so there are a very few of them left in the market as of now. We have asked the company to withdraw the entire batch currently in the market,"* said Khobargade. In December 2006, the company announced that the cost of dealing with the contamination would reach £30 million.

A focused and intense communications program was implemented over the next six months to rebuild credibility and restore confidence among the key stakeholders. In a damage-control exercise, appropriately called "PROJECT

VISHWAS" Cadbury India announced a three-step strategic program involving its packaging, distribution chain and retail channels. For the first time in 30 years, the company is discontinuing the system of loose sales for Cadbury Dairy Milk range and changing its outer package.

In media, the key message communicated, infestation was a storage-linked problem, not manufacturing related, found widespread acceptance. Across the board, media carried Cadbury's point-of-view on the issue. Sales volumes climbed back to pre-crisis levels eight weeks after the launch of new packaging, a good step taken by the company to minimize the incidence of infestation. This reflected consumer confidence in the brand and the company.

Conclusion

In conclusion, Cadbury is one of the world best brands with growing potential for growth. Managers at Cadbury need to recognize existing advantage base of analyze the competitive environment they operate in and internal strengths. Cadbury need to capitalize on existing opportunities the emerging presenting and the growth of middle-class and rising income of the Indian population. Cadbury can also work on their cost reduction further to increase profitability and further improve their marketing channels. Product innovation through technology enhancement will continue to be a priority to Cadbury.

References

Anderson, R. H., Bilson, T. K., Law, S. A., & Mitchell, B. M. (2017). Abelson, R."In a crisis, Coke tries to be reassuring." The New York Times. June 16, 1999, www. nytimes. com/1999/06/16/business/in-a-crisis-coke-tries-to-be-reassuring. html. Achaya, KT Indian Food: A Historical Companion. 1994. Oxford University Press. 1998. *The English Paradigm in India: Essays in Language, Literature and Culture*, 293.

Grant, R. M. (2016). *Contemporary strategy analysis: Text and cases edition*. John Wiley & Sons.

Kaul, A., & Desai, A. (2017). Building Reputational Bridges Over Crises Situations. In *The English Paradigm in India* (pp. 265-284). Palgrave Macmillan, Singapore.

Baral, S. K. (2017). A Critical Study on Corporate Social Responsibility (CSR) Models in India. *Splint International Journal of Professionals*, *4*(5), 74-85.

Areal, A., McIntosh, B., & Sheppy, B. (2016). Hope and glory: an expanded social strategy diagnosis model to incorporate corporate social responsibility within business strategy. *International Journal of Business Performance Management*, *17*(2), 117-131.

Telang, A., & Deshpande, A. (2016). Keep calm and carry on: A crisis communication study of Cadbury and McDonalds. *Management & Marketing*, *11*(1), 371-379.

Bernstein, H., & Brass, T. (2016). Globalisation and Restructuring in the Indian Food Industry. In *Agrarian Questions* (pp. 199-218). Routledge.

Park, S. H., Ungson, G. R., & Cosgrove, A. (2015). Co-aligning Strategies with Management Structures and Systems. In *Scaling the Tail: Managing Profitable Growth in Emerging Markets* (pp. 91-107). Palgrave Pivot, New York.

Thach, S., Unni, R., & Abdelmoety, Z. (2018). Local Brands and Global Brands: Competition in Emerging Markets.

QATAR AIRWAYS (QATAR)

Company Background

Qatar Airways (QA) was rated as the world's No. 1 Airlines in year 2015. Qatar Airways is founded in year 1993 and it has been fully controlled and run by the government since July 2013. QA hub is based in Doha, Qatar with divisions including; Qatar Aircraft Catering Company, Doha International Airport, Qatar Airways Holidays, United Media International, Qatar Duty Free, Qatar Aviation Services, Qatar Distribution Company, and Qatar Executive.

Operating in a highly competitive environment, QA has managed to expand with averaging of 30% growth year to year, and flying one of the most modern fleet of 158 aircrafts. Qatar Airways won awards such as Airline of the Year, Best Business Class Airline Seat and Best Airline in the Middle East, at the 2015 Skytrax Awards. This is the third time the airline won the accolade of Airline of the Year. QA plans to establish a worldwide cargo hub and is pushing towards high value products and services targeting corporate and affluent travelers.

Business Model

QA aspires to be the best, in newest and youngest fleets airplane in the sky, and reach the pinnacle of the airline industry for outstanding in-flight service, superior onboard products, and operational excellence. QA has a reasonable cost base yet offers luxury products and services. If an airline provides better price offers with top quality products and services, others cannot easily compete with it, but its profit margin suffers.

QA provides five-star luxury business class cabins that worth for consumers. QA read the minds of high-end consumers where QA not only ordered luxury interior airplanes. When consumers arrive to the newly constructed Doha airport, QA intend to make travelers feel special and impress them with unique sense of design, quality of surrounding environment such as endless wine list in the dining area, white marble, and abundance of fresh flowers.

The beauty of business class helps international travelers to ease jetlag and fatigue with options like the luxurious spa and showers at the business class lounge. Serving as a hub for international travelers, connecting Australia, Asia, Middle East to Europe and the Americas, travelers immediately feel the value money when benchmarked with other airlines. This experience can also be felt with major neighboring competitors such as Etihad Airlines and Emirate Airlines. However, QA's strategic objective is to create brand loyalty with their passengers.

During 2015, QA was made aware that streaming is the way to go for In-Flight Entertainment (IFE) system in the future. As such, QA launched Oryx One, an enhanced interface for its inflight entertainment (IFE) system where a device set at the back of seat to let all passengers to use while they get bored in the sky such as increasing the number of movies and TV shows on board from 950 to up to 2,000 in individual screen. QA airplanes also offer advanced LED mood lighting and air conditioning technology to enhance the comfort of passengers in an effort to reduce travel fatigue.

Moreover, QA airplanes also offer inflight WiFi connectivity for all passengers allowing them to surf the web on the go. This added to the competitive advantages QA enjoys. QA predicted that within the next five to seven years, passengers would have their own smart devices on board, where they'll have the option of fixing it onto the seat and use the IFE in plane system to enjoy various online resources, media subscriptions and enjoy email services.

QA uniqueness also lies in the routs thy fly such as the popular non-stop flights from Doha to Nagpur, India and Doha to Osaka, Japan. QA is keen on targeting business class passengers, who are generally willing to pay more for nonstop flight to save time. QA aims to service growth destinations to further develop their competitive advantage.

Nagpur, India and Tokyo, Japan are such successful routs. Leisure and business travelers from Nagpur for instance, can now experience enhanced connectivity to more than 150 international destinations through seamless connections via the newly opened Doha's Hamad International Airport.

Furthermore, QA managed to be the first 'Business Aviation Operator' in the Middle-East and one of first worldwide to be awarded the European Aviation Safety Agency's (EASA) third-country operator (TCO) safety certificate.

This safety certificate was rated as the most significant certification during 2016. Non-EU commercial operators wishing to fly to Europe, will be required to hold this safety standard certification. With number of air crash accidents during 2015, such as Malaysia airlines and Asia Airlines, QA capitalizes on the concern of passengers through an outstanding safety records in addition to the added airport security, which is considered to be a top priority for the airlines. QA is aware of the importance of continuous improvement, and as such, they put enormous effort in enhancing international safety standards to achieve the rapid growth network development.

Moreover, QA is constantly willing to invest in new aircrafts and pilot training programs to avoid airplane accidents. In May, 2015, QA placed an order for 30 new aircraft from Gulfstream Aerospace Corp. Cabin crew are highly trained and chosen from over 112 countries to be able to communicate with the diverse nationality of travelers by speaking their own languages.

QA newly opened airport exhibits creative art, culturally divers work and shopping elements. In 2015, QA opened at Hamad International Airport in Doha, a new Qatar Duty Free gift shops, high-end cafes and a museum. When visiting the newly opened airport, passengers get the opportunity to learn something about Qatar and its culture through museums exhibits. The objective is to allow passengers to to experience QA hospitality and high level of travel luxury. This is represented in the uniqueness of cafes and restaurants, designed to impress by hexagonal texture flooring, a three dimensional ceiling and mix of copper varnished metal, old grey oak, back painted glass padded benches and chairs in the airport's public areas, all of which aims to provide passengers with special feel of unique travel experience.

To maintain their competitive advantage, QA is continuously investing in enhancing the level of air travel efficiency through fuel optimization programs. This is also communicated directly with airplane manufacturers such as Boeing and Airbus. The world's two largest aircraft manufacturers; namely Boeing and Airbus, put special emphases on the issue fuel efficiency to reduce fuel cost to various airlines, which immediately impacts airlines profitability. This is doe through rigorous R&D process that involves continuous testing and implementation of new methods and technologies to reduce carbon emissions. This process is heavily impacted by reduction in aircraft weight, which has a direct impact on fuel consumption. This process of efficiency optimization takes into consideration impact on flight routes, and use of energy while taxiing to and from runway. A main contributor to profitability however remains the government fuel subsidy. Qatar as a main producer of oil and gas helps QA through various programs including special price of fuel supply. QA however helps the small state to increase the number of visitors and improve tourism to the country.

Future Challenge

There is a mounting pressure on QA to continue to play a crucial role in global aviation industry. With low oil prices and decreasing willingness to provide government subsidies, QA is required to be more profitable in the face of mounting regional competition by Etihad and Emirate airlines, in addition to global competition by international carriers. The natures of competition between QA and emirate airlines lead to cannibalization of market share. Both operators are fighting for the same market share and market segments.

QA like Emirates airlines continue to target and attracts the affluent business travelers, by constantly improving their offering of luxury services. A diversification in routs between QA and Emirates is needed. A further cooperation in joint flights might help both airlines to service different routs and thus create operational efficiency. In 2016, QA announced further expansion in operations to include more destinations such as Los Angeles, Boston and Atlanta in USA, Ras Al Khaimah in UAE, Sydney and Adelaide in Australia, and Birmingham in UK.

Finally, such expansion puts more pressure on profitability margins and infrastructure challenges in addition to shortages of pilots, adequate staffing, compliance with safety and aviation standards and other issues that impacts operational cost in times of more competition from neighboring rivals of major carriers such as Etihad Airways and Emirates Airlines.

References

Lohmann, G., & Spasojevic, B. (2018). Airline business strategy. *The Routledge Companion to Air Transport Management*, 139.

Chiambaretto, P., & Wassmer, U. (2018). Resource utilization as an internal driver of alliance portfolio evolution: the Qatar airways case (1993–2010). *Long Range Planning*.

SET, S. (1933). THE AGENCY.

O'Connell, J. F. (2011). The rise of the Arabian Gulf carriers: An insight into the business model of Emirates Airline. *Journal of Air Transport Management, 17*(6), 339-346.

Hazime, H. (2011). From city branding to e-brands in developing countries: An approach to Qatar and Abu Dhabi. *African Journal of Business Management, 5*(12).

Alrawi, K. W., & Sabry, K. A. (2009). E-commerce evolution: a Gulf region review. *International Journal of Business Information Systems, 4*(5), 509-526.

McKechnie, D. S., Grant, J., & Katsioloudes, M. (2008). Positions and positioning: strategy simply stated. *Business strategy series, 9*(5), 224-230.

Heracleous, L., & Wirtz, J. (2012). Strategy and organisation at Singapore Airlines: achieving sustainable advantage through dual strategy. In *Energy, Transport, & the Environment*(pp. 479-493). Springer, London.

Kedia, B. L., & Lahiri, S. (2007). International outsourcing of services: A partnership model. *Journal of International Management, 13*(1), 22-37.

Stark, J. (2015). Product lifecycle management. In *Product Lifecycle Management (Volume 1)* (pp. 1-29). Springer, Cham.

Lange, K., Geppert, M., Saka-Helmhout, A., & Becker-Ritterspach, F. (2015). Changing business models and employee representation in the airline industry: a comparison of British Airways and Deutsche Lufthansa. *British Journal of Management, 26*(3), 388-407.

Dunn, S. (2002). Down to business on climate change: an overview of corporate strategies. *GSE Research*, 10.

Zamir, Z., Sahar, A., & Zafar, F. (2014). Strategic alliances; A comparative analysis of successful alliances in large and medium scale enterprises around the world. *Educational Research International*, *3*(1), 25-39.

Conventz, S., Thierstein, A., Wiedmann, F., & Salama, A. M. (2015). When the Oryx takes off: Doha a new rising knowledge hub in the Gulf region?. *International Journal of Knowledge-Based Development*, *6*(1), 65-82.

Thomas, H., Smith, R. R., & Diez, F. (2013). *Human capital and global business strategy*. Cambridge University Press.

TESLA (U.S.A.)

Company Background

Tesla is fairly new company with the business model to design "manly" and energy efficient cars. This model is very capital intensive and requires sophisticated minute factoring capabilities, something which is Tesla still trying to achieve burning almost $1 billion Per quarter (Bloomberg, February 24, 2017). This was electric cars are differentiated from other cars since it is completely electric and consider to be a new concept in the marketplace. Demand has shown to be very strong for such cars, however keeping up with demand is the problem. Tesla's manufacturing capabilities are modest and requires tesla to go to the capital markets regularly asking for money to build manufacturing capabilities to me in such high demand.

This is creating a problem for tesla because they must be able to show profits, which they haven't done so yet.

Investors would like to see a light at the end of the tunnel by getting a return on their investment rather than continue to pour money into a business model that is not showing profits as of yet. Tesla has only three models, the second model-T was very successful since a regulation introduced by president Obama helped Tesla significantly, by giving tax breaks to model T buyers (Bloomberg, February 24, 2017). The third model of Tesla is proved to be the most successful because of the large demand for it. However, Tesla could not keep up with production and had to return money to those customers waiting for up to 2 years to get their model 3. Production capacity is something that's Tesla continues to struggle with. Although Tesla's business model differs from other traditional automotive manufacturers, in the way that it relies on the electric technology it creates an attempt to mass-produce vehicles that would force their competitors to do the same or risk being out of business.

It is important to remember that Tesla's competitors already own large manufacturing base with well established distribution networks, well capitalized companies, will establish repetitions, and well-established brand name amongst consumers (Bloomberg Technology 23 February

2017). This is the competitive landscape that will continue to challenge the Tesla's business model. Initially Tesla is attempting to capitalize on paving and serving a niche by distinguishing themselves as high-performance electric luxury supporters.

The Business Model

This helped to transform the company and demand for model T. However, innovation is supposed to drive Tesla's business model in a new direction. The third model which is anticipated to hit the markets soon (Bloomberg Technology 23 February 2017) supposed to generate enough profits to make Tesla's business model viable to investors, because they will be shift in the business model from high end luxury carmaker to more of a generic and cars for everyone kind of company, similar to that of the main existing automakers. As such, Tesla will continue to go back to capital markets asking for more money the strength their manufacturing base to keep up with increasing consumer demand for their T model, and to successfully achieve the new shift in their business model. This will also cause Tesla to demand more capital from investors to successfully realize such business model.

Amongst other challenges to the new business model of Tesla is the lack of adequate infrastructure required for successfully compete with other car makers. Tesla is in the process of establishing a retail dealership network, which they lack currently, to improve sales of the newly anticipated third generation car model. This however is time consuming. Tesla is mainly a battery company with the idea to venture in the automotive industry.

It is a huge gamble from Tesla's part to build a business model that competes with giants such as GM Mercedes BMW or Toyota. All these companies, in addition to European automakers have a huge budget for research and development and have been exploring energy efficient cars and electric energy for at least two decades now. Even companies such as Google and Apple are successfully exploring and experimenting in the fully electric energy efficient vehicle for the past few years. This provides Tesla with even greater challenges when considering the number of automakers already in the marketplace with capabilities to mimic Tesla's model.

Conclusion

Although the market for electric vehicle is experiencing a great growth largely because of the safety regulations, advances in electric technology, global positioning systems (GPS), computing power, governmental desire to reduce emission through tighter regulations and most importantly consumers' awareness of the importance of energy efficient vehicles such as electric cars. The fundamental bedrock of Tesla's business model remains the innovation of batteries. It is important to mention that Tesla license many of their technologies (Bergen, M. 24 February 2017) and still heavily dependent on the vision of their CEO Elon Musk to see this company a successful one. In fact, many of their investors are not sure whether to sell Tesla's stocks or whether they should hold on to their shares in hope it will pay off in the long run (Bloomberg, February 24, 2017). However, in final analysis, the future of Tesla remains completely ambiguous.

References

Bloomberg, February 24, 2017. *Lucid Motors Aims to Rival Tesla*

Bergen, M. 24 February 2017. *Ambitious Engineer at Center of Colossal Fight Between Google and Uber.* Bloomberg

Dana Hull and David Welch. *Tesla Is Burning Through Cash*, Bloomberg Technology 23 February 2017

Rothaermel, F. T. (2015). *Strategic management.* McGraw-Hill Education.

Bohnsack, R., Pinkse, J., & Kolk, A. (2014). Business models for sustainable technologies: Exploring business model evolution in the case of electric vehicles. *Research Policy, 43*(2), 284-300.

Porter, M. E., & Heppelmann, J. E. (2015). How smart, connected products are transforming companies. *Harvard Business Review, 93*(10), 96-114.

Lei, D., & Slocum Jr, J. W. (2009). The Tipping Points of Business Strategy:: The Rise and Decline of Competitiveness. *Organizational Dynamics, 38*(2), 131-147.

Halal, W. E. (2015). Business strategy for the technology revolution: competing at the edge of creative destruction. *Journal of the Knowledge Economy, 6*(1), 31-47.

Wieland, H., Hartmann, N. N., & Vargo, S. L. (2017). Business models as service strategy. *Journal of the Academy of Marketing Science, 45*(6), 925-943.

Chen, Y., & Perez, Y. (2017). Business model design: lessons learned from Tesla Motors.

LEGO

Company Background

LEGO is the fastest growing toy maker in the world, was established in the city of Billund, Denmark during 1932. However, over the past ten years, the company started loosing one million dollars in revenues a day. Toys are not the main revenue source for LEGO. By 2004, LEGO owned over 50 video games, movies, theme parks and retail stores.

The Problem in the Business Model

Although LEGO created the construction segment of the toy market, LEGO lost its focus on its core business and was on the brink of collapse. In a broader sense, LEGO has lost its identity according to its CEO Vig Knudstorp. LEGO needed to redefine their existence through a process of re-identifying their core business by asking what makes

LEGO unique? What value they provide to the consumer, and what they really sell? LEGO did not only loose their understanding of their core business, they also underestimated the power of their brand and lacked the understanding of their own strengths.

To save the company, LEGO hired a former Mckinsey Consultant Jorgen Vig Knudstorp as a CEO to help turn the company around. In fact, his turn around of LEGO was one of the best corporate turn around of the century. Knudstorp was the first CEO from outside the original founding family. So he went on company sole searching to redefine the purpose of their existence, business model and business operations.

Knudstorp describes his initial assessment of LEGO as lack of understanding of the profit structures of operations, in terms of how they made profits, and where profits might be generated. Additionally, Knudstorp described LEGO as lacking strategic corporate discipline in terms of poor forecasting, communications between stores, poor operational processes such as data sharing and absence of compatibility between manufacturing and forecasting, lack of adequate assessment of which customers are the profitable ones. The complexity of LEGO illustrated in the vertical integration of its operations, which significantly contributed to loss of focus and the rise of financial problems as a direct result of such complexity. LEGO's expansion into theme parks, clothing, books, and video games proved to be disastrous, since LEGO had no prior experience in running such ventures. By 2004, Morgan Stanly a partial owner of LEGO attempted to sell their stake in LEGO because of the bad performance and constant loss of revenues.

The solution

LEGO needed to streamline its operations, simplify their business model and re-prioritize their operations. With Knudstorp as new CEO, LEGO had to downsize and sell off some business units such as theme parks. In an effort of re-scoping and reorganizing LEGO, the new CEO also streamlined product manufacturing from 13,000 elements to 7,000. During the reorganization period to reviving LEGO as a company, sales dropped by 25% in 2004, which was very difficult for stakeholders to accept, only to see sales grow again by 5% during 2005 when Knudstorp efforts started to pay off in reviving LEGO.

Capitalizing on LEGO's brand equity, the company went back to their fans to see what they like and what they want. As part of reinventing themselves, LEGO went on inventing new products and product lines. LEGO had to refocus their effort on their core advantages and maximizing leverage of the LEGO brand. Knudstorp's advice was to reconnect with loyal consumer base to rediscover the secret of LEGO's attraction to consumers. The annual conference of LEGO fans was the perfect opportunity to connect with LEGO lovers and attempt to learn more about what customers liked about LEGO, wanted from LEGO and how they can contribute to LEGO's improvement. Fans and customers provided all kinds of suggestions and recommendations that proved to be invaluable to the company.

Business Model

LEGO also went about opening up the company by explaining how they make their products, and as a result, ended up hiring some of their fans. This journey of rediscovery of what is LEGO is all about also included the involvement of retailers and suppliers. As a result, Knudstorp went about redefining LEGO as "A material that is endlessly creative with endless possibilities to create creative things with imagination". The refocus on production, product innovation and strong marketing research, helped LEGO to regain their profitability and quadruple its revenues. In 2013, LEGO manufactured 55 billion LEGO pieces in one year. LEGO was asking children consumers over four years what they would like to have as new products. Knowing that an early gift of LEGO in early stages of childhood would develop a loyal customer for life.

Today, LEGO is expanding into untapped segments of growing markets in Asia, Africa & Latin America. Utilizing cheaper labor and improving distribution in those regions, in attempt to be the first in the market with new fashionable toys and ideas. LEGO profit margins in 2013 were up by 24%, over taking its two largest rivals Mattel and Hasbro. LEGO's story is not only a story of success through reinventing themselves, reshaping the organization, rediscovering the purpose of their existence, but it's the story of the importance of top management role in shaping corporate success or failure.

References

El Sawy, O. A., Kræmmergaard, P., Amsinck, H., & Vinther, A. L. (2016). How LEGO Built the Foundations and Enterprise Capabilities for Digital Leadership. *MIS Quarterly Executive, 15*(2).

Luo, Z., & Pollack, R. (1992). *LEGO proof development system: User's manual*. LFCS, Department of Computer Science, University of Edinburgh.

Schultz, M., & Hatch, M. J. (2003). The cycles of corporate branding: The case of the LEGO company. *California Management Review, 46*(1), 6-26.

Eilers, S. (2016). The LEGO Counting Problem. *The American Mathematical Monthly, 123*(5), 415-426.

Hatch, M. J., & Schultz, M. (2001). Are the strategic stars aligned for your corporate brand. *Harvard business review, 79*(2), 128-134.

Hansen, M. T., Nohria, N., & Tierney, T. (1999). What's your strategy for managing knowledge. *The knowledge management yearbook 2000–2001*, 1-10.

Osterwalder, A., Pigneur, Y., & Tucci, C. L. (2005). Clarifying business models: Origins, present, and future of the concept. *Communications of the association for Information Systems, 16*(1), 1.

Eisenhardt, K. M., & Sull, D. N. (2001). Strategy as simple rules. *Harvard business review, 79*(1), 106-119.

Grant, R. M. (2016). *Contemporary strategy analysis: Text and cases edition*. John Wiley & Sons.

Firend, A. R., & Langroudi, M. (2016). Co-creation and consumer's purchasing intentions, any value in B2B activities?. *Journal of Life Science and Biotechnology, 1*(4), 133-141.

Chang, J. F. (2016). *Business process management systems: strategy and implementation*. CRC Press.

Nadeem, A., Abedin, B., Cerpa, N., & Chew, E. (2018). digital transformation & digital business strategy in electronic commerce-the role of organizational capabilities. *Journal of Theoretical and Applied Electronic Commerce Research, 13*(2), I-VIII.

WALT DISNEY

Company Background

The Walt Disney Company or, as everyone know the company as "Disney" is a U.S. based company, founded in 1923. Disney operates internationally and is in a diversified mass media and entertainment industry. Disney's headquarters is in Burbank, California and is known as the Walt Disney Studios. Disney managed to establish itself as one of the leaders in the animation industry in USA before venturing into theme parks, live action film production and television. Disney has also operated under the names of The Walt Disney Studio and Walt Disney Productions before taking on its current name, The Walt Disney Company.

Business Model

Disney's business model revolves around several types of businesses. It includes media networks that comprises of a vast variety of cable, broadcast, radio, digital businesses and publishing (Disney/ABC Television Group and ESPN Inc), parks and resorts that are one of the world's leading providers of leisure experiences and family travel (Disneyland Hong Kong, Disneyland Tokyo, Disneyland Paris, Tokyo Disney Resort, Disneyland Resort, Disney Cruise Line, Etc), studio entertainment where for almost 90 years, The Walt Disney Studios have brought quality music, songs, movie and even stage plays to people around the world (Walt Disney Animation Studios, Pixar Animation Studios, Disneytoon Studios, Disney Theatrical Group, etc.), Disney consumer merchandise where Disney characters are brought to life in the forms of toys, apparels, arts, books and many more and finally, Disney interactive where high quality interactive entertainments are created across digital and media platforms through console games and virtual worlds that are online (Disney Official Website, n.d.).

All of these have clearly generated billions of revenues for Disney. Disney generates its revenue from few streams. The first being its media businesses networks where affiliate fees are charges to satellite, cable and telecommunication service providers that are affiliated with Disney's broadcasting network in the US, advertising fees during commercial breaks, and the sale of DVDs, Blu-ray disks and sales from online stores.

The second being through its parks and resorts businesses where fees that are collected upon admission, sales of food, beverage and merchandise from theme parks, charges for rooms in hotels and sales of cruise packages. The third, being from its studio entertainment business where revenues are generated from the distribution of films to consumer worldwide. Fourth being from its consumer merchandise businesses where characters of Disney are sold all around the world through their physical store as well as their online stores. Lastly, Disney's revenues come from its interactive businesses where their games are sold, through subscription to and in-game transactions for mobile and online games as well as from online advertising.

Disney's value or its key strengths lies in its very diverse portfolio that includes animation, sports and movie channels using renounced brands like ABS, Walt Disney, ABC, Marvel Entertainment, Lucasfilm and Touchstone

Pictures. Its diversity helps Disney to reduce risk in a way that it will equalize or maintain balance when future revenues faces loss in the DVD segment due to piracy or having other cheaper viewing alternatives (Kehoe, 2014). Disneyland has proven to be Disney's crown jewel because the franchises and characters across various platforms are hard to replicate. This makes Disney different from others and for consumers to experience all the magical moments, they can only turn to Disney. This in turn has become one of Disney's competitive advantages in the market.

Up to this point, it is obvious that Disney's key activities are producing and distributing films, movies, theatrical and merchandise, marketing and managing their brand worldwide as well as tourism activities through their cruises, theme parks and resorts. Its distribution channels on the other hand are through theme parks, resorts, televisions, cinemas, online, theaters and even through the webs.

This allows Disney to reach a wide range of customers internationally without boundaries. Customers have proven to play an essential part in Disney's growth. Their customer segmentations have no boundaries. It travels from kids to teenager to even adults due to the diversity of its products and services provided. From animations to live action movies, all customers from different age groups are drawn to awe with their diverse productions. For example, Disney's Frozen has generated approximately $1.27 billion and more than $1billion in the sales of merchandise as they managed to make generations of kids as well as adults dream of the imaginary world (Amarsy, 2015).

Disney also expands its reach through its strategic partners and alliance. One of which, is PANDORA Jewelry where Disney characters are made into charms and are fitted into the charm bracelets that are PANDORA's main product. Another strategic alliance that has proven to be a success is with Hewlett Packard since 1937 when Disney himself bought a customized oscillator that was made by Bill Hewlett and David Packard in their garage.

Today, Disney and HP are celebrating their years of strategic alliance and Disney is giving HP an arrangement that is worth $50 to $60 million a year (Granstedt, 2014). Their most well known collaboration is Mission SPACE, where it is a simulation of a trip to Mars. HP had also created devises that provide translations and subtitles to non-English speaking guests when they go for certain rides and attractions. Disney however realizing the importance of on-demand media such as Netflix, and Amazon Prime, Disney is attempting to start their own on-demand channel subscription and application to compete in the digital media era.

References

Wasko, J. (2016). The Walt Disney Company. In *Global Media Giants* (pp. 25-39). Routledge.

Thomas, B. (2017). *Walt Disney: An American Original*. Disney Electronic Content.

Yamaguchi, R. (2018). The Walt Disney Company vs Studio Ghibli: Exploring the Possibility to Achieve Both Artistic and Commercial Successes in the Mainstream Animation Industry.

Becker, C. (2017). The Magic Behind the Magic: Discovering why The Walt Disney Company is so Successful.

Wilson, S. (2017). Personnel Strategy for Multinational Firms: A Case Study of the Walt Disney Company in China. *Asian Political Science Review*, *1*(1), 65-70.

Huddleston, G. S., Garlen, J. C., & Sandlin, J. A. (2016). A New Dimension of Disney Magic: MyMagic+ and Controlled Leisure.

Sull, D., Turconi, S., Sull, C., & Yoder, J. (2018). Four Logics of Corporate Strategy. *MIT Sloan Management Review*, *59*(2), 136-142.

Kane, G. C., Palmer, D., Phillips, A. N., Kiron, D., & Buckley, N. (2015). Strategy, not technology, drives digital transformation. *MIT Sloan Management Review and Deloitte University Press*, *14*.

Wilson, S. (2017). Personnel Strategy for Multinational Firms: A Case Study of the Walt Disney Company in China. *Asian Political Science Review*, *1*(1), 65-70.

Lillestol, T., Timothy, D. J., & Goodman, R. (2015). Competitive strategies in the US theme park industry: a popular media perspective. *International Journal of Culture, Tourism and Hospitality Research, 9*(3), 225-240.

11STREET'S BUSINESS MODEL

Company Background

11street is South Korean company that partnered with Celcom Planet of Malaysia in November 2014, as a joint venture between a Malaysian company, Celcom Axiata Bhd. and the South Korean ecommerce online marketplace provider SK Planet Ltd. 11street is first established in South Korea in 2008 and then Turkey known as n11 and Indonesia known as elevenia.

Business Model

11street's business model is to introduce guaranteed lowest price of their products, sold through their website. 11street provides discounted prices on brand names and known quality products. They promise that if the customer is able to locate the same product selling at cheaper price at another online shopping website, 11street will refund the consumers with the price difference of the product at 110%. Through 11street, buyers can purchase quality low-priced brands and products when compared with prices at the local shopping mall. With the introduction of Goods & Services Tax "GST" in Malaysia and the new implementation of Value Added Taxes "VAT" in Korea, 11street becomes very attractive option for shoppers.

The uniqueness of 11street offerings is that it provides a good mixture of local and global brands. 11street is able to deliver to their consumers' popular brands and products from around the world, especially Korea, Japan and Taiwan to enrich local consumers' shopping experience at competitive prices. As such, buyers need not to worry about comparing prices online, and save on travel cost by purchasing directly from 11street. A buying experience is being created here and shopping convenience while payments made in local currencies.

11street also highlighted that their partner Celcom's products are available for consumers to grab at their official websites, since 11street is in joint venture with Celcom and SK Planet. Thus, 11street can attract Celcom's loyal customers to browse their website. The fact that Celcom is popular in Malaysia and SK Planet is popular in Korea, a sense of trustworthiness is created here for both the seller and buyers.

Another competitive advantage is that it will be the first online shopping website in Malaysia that promotes not only physical products but also deal offerings such as e-vouchers. The e-vouchers can be a gift any consumer can buy and give it a friend or family to purchase what they like. This is a form of indirect introduction of 11street to more shoppers and deliver greater satisfaction and rewarding online shopping experience.

In 2015, 11street invested RM35 million (about $8 mill. USD) in various marketing programs, seller development and promotions to bring local sellers on-board and to attract new consumers to their website. [4] In 2016, the strategic team plans to invite at least 11,000 sellers on-board to ensure the delivery of trendy and enriched shopping experience packed with a diverse range of products and services. [4]

11street designed online merchandizing tools called 'Seller Zone'. It is one of the costliest investments that 11street ever made to help grow Malaysia's e-commerce. It will be the first e-commerce education center where e-commerce seminars and workshops will be provided to educate the masses on how e-commerce operates. Sellers especially are of interest to 11street such as housewives or anyone interested to work from home, will be able to understand the mechanism of e-commerce during the seminar sessions. Some of the 11street partners conducting the training sessions includes Malaysia's national ICT agency Multimedia Development Corporate (MDeC) and Google Malaysia. 11street also provides professional photography studios to assist seller who are not able to do product shooting themselves. Since product image is very important element in online shopping experience, sellers will be taught how to upload attractive pictures of their offerings to draw attention and to compete with competitors. The center will be equipped with free WiFi for the public, and open zone cafeteria for networking and relaxation.

Another element 11street providing is early bird promotion packages for those who register with their website before April 2015. Extra benefit and bonus has been given such as no store fee, 50 per cent discount on transaction fee, promotion credits, complimentary use of "seller zone" facilities and product listing coupons. Mobility trends suggests that 11street offers an integrated application and mobile interface on their websites to create convenience to sellers, and the ability to manage their stocks, payment settlements, and marketing programs. In order to compete, 11street released the mobile apps in both iOS and Android smartphones. In just few years in Korea, 11street created a proven track record such as backdrop. These similar approach will be adopted to help Malaysian online sellers to excel in today's increasingly competitive e-commerce market space.

During the first launched event, 11street introduced the iconic Korean pop artists, which are popular across Asia such as the famous actor Lee Min Ho and Malaysian actress Emily Chan. Such strategic move is to attract sellers and buyer through their fans base to create awareness. 11street's today has become No.1 online marketplace in S. Korea and Turkey are ranked No 2 in Indonesia's online shopping market. 11street was able to detect changes and trends in consumer needs and build their business model creatively around such trends. Capitalizing on Generation "Y" (kids born in 1980's-1990s and electronically savvy) savviness in social media and the digital world, internet shopping through smartphone devices is the preferred choice of future large segment of the population, which is growing by the hour, especially in Asia.

References

Cavusgil, S. T., Knight, G., Riesenberger, J. R., Rammal, H. G., & Rose, E. L. (2014). *International business*. Pearson Australia.

Barney, J. B. (2014). *Gaining and sustaining competitive advantage*. Pearson higher ed.

Cavusgil, S. T., & Knight, G. (2015). The born global firm: An entrepreneurial and capabilities perspective on early and rapid internationalization. *Journal of International Business Studies*, *46*(1), 3-16.

Wheelen, T. L., Hunger, J. D., Hoffman, A. N., & Bamford, C. E. (2015). *Concepts in Strategic Management and Business Policy*. Pearson.

https://www.digitalnewsasia.com/startups/11street-goes-live-in-malaysia?page=2

http://www.kpopstarz.com/articles/196200/20150427/lee-minho-met-with-fans-in-malaysia-as-11street-brand-ambassador.htm

http://www.businesscircle.com.my/11street-bets-big-on-malaysia/

http://www.marketingmagazine.com.my/breaking-news/11-000-for-11street-rm35m-invested-in-malaysia

http://www.koreatimes.co.kr/www/news/biz/2008/04/123_19653.html

Singapore Airlines

Company Background

Singapore Airlines is a Singaporean company that commenced operation in 1972. Over the last two decades, Singapore Airlines has grown from a regional airline into one of the world's finest passenger and cargo carriers. Singapore Airlines owns a modern and young fleet of aircrafts. Based in *Changi* Airport, which is considered as one of the world's best, serves as the gateway to Asia and the rest of the world.

Background

They have come a long way from their humble origins as a small regional airline. Their story began in 1947, when Malayan Airways first operated a twin-engine Airspeed Consul between Singapore, Kuala Lumpur, Ipoh and Penang. Passenger demand grew and so did the fledging airline. By 1955 it had a fleet of Duoglas DC-3s. The creation of the Federation of Malaysia in 1963 prompted two name changes; first to Malaysian Airways and then, three years later, to Malaysia-Singapore Airlines (MSA) in deference to the carrier's joint shareholders, the governments of Malaysia and Singapore.

MSA ceased operations in October 1972 and two new airlines, Malaysia Airline System (now called Malaysia Airlines) and Singapore Airlines, were born. At its launch, the new national flag carrier of Singapore had a modest fleet comprising 10 aircraft, a staff of 6000 and route network spanning 22 cities in 18 countries. It also had 25 years of experience and boundless ambition. Singapore Airlines immediately began to expand and modernize its fleet, setting standards of service that others could only follow. Far-sighted planning, investment and product innovation propelled its growing reputation and profitability. The little airline from the small island state in Asia became big

Business Model

Singaporean Airlines (SIA) grow its business as cost leader and premium service provider. The strategy for there business model is to enhance customer service and improve product offering to meet and satisfy customers demand instead of adopting cost saving concept usually implemented by other traditional airlines. Singaporean Airlines strongly attempted to improve their business by maintaining their status as a premium airline, connect passengers between busy and main destinations, and provide a unique and comfortable experience.

Over the past four decades, SIA earned a reputation in the high competitive commercial aviation business by providing customers with high-quality service and dominating the business-travel segments at competitive prices. This strategy was proven right when SIA won the World's Best Airline award from Condé Nast Traveller 21 out of the 22 times it has been awarded and Skytrax's Airline of the year award three times over the past ten years.

SIA adopts a customer-focused model instead of focusing on competitors. Although Singaporean Airlines services involves high operational cost, yet they managed to maintain healthy profit margins. The core of their strategy focuses on taking financial risks (high investments) in an effort to offer best customer service, which will yield better profit in the long-run. SIA was among the first in Asian airlines to focus on superior customer service experience and enhancing its reputation by providing superior services at competitive prices.

This in turn helped SIA to maintain sustainable competitive advantage in the global airlines industry, particularly in Asia where it connects people between various continents. To achieve premium positioning and cost-effective excellence in service, they look at their core philosophy, which lies at the heat of their business model is their view that the two most important assets they possess is the fleet and people. Both assets must be able to provide a service better than rivals.

To that effect, SIA ensure that its fleet is always young. For instance, in 2009, aircrafts were 74 months old on average, hence, all planes are less than half the industry average of 160 months. This strategy helped maintain low mechanical cost, fewer takeoff delays, more arrivals are on time, and fewer flight cancellation. New airplanes tend to be more fuel-efficient as they need less repair and maintenance.

All these factors, played an important role in shaping their excellent in service and placing customers at the center of their business model. Singapore Airlines aircraft spend less time in hangars, which means more time in the air, an average of 13 hours a day, as oppose to 11.3 hours a day industry average. Air travelers always appreciate newer airplanes, this double edge strategy helped both the airline to realize cost savings, and customers to appreciate better and newer aircrafts and travel experience *(The Globe: Singapore Airlines' Balancing Act; Loizos Heracleous and Jochen Wirtz, 2010)*. Being aware of the importance of training, Singapore Airlines invests heavily in training and development of their air and ground crew. Newly recruited staff are hand picked through rigorous process, and spend an average of four months in training compared with an average of eight weeks by other airlines in Asia. Training includes courses on a wide range of activities ranging from etiquette to wine appreciation and cultural sensitivity.

Trainees learn to manage various issues raised by passengers, such as communicating at eye level rather than "talking down" to passengers by kneeling down to be at the seat level of the passenger when conversing. The resulting superior service not only delights customers, but also helps improve profits through the spread of word of mouth and maximizing passenger turnover. High-level training created a feedback system whereby cabin crews found that about one third of passengers don't eat dinner on late-night flights out of Singapore. And so, they recommended carrying less food on board.

Singapore Airlines offers two brands of champagne in first class, and spends $8 million on champagne annually. In their constant attempt to maintain lower cost, cabin crew constantly attempt to minimize waste by pouring from whichever open champagne bottle, unless a passenger specifically requests the other brand. The airlines also decided recently not to place jam jars on every breakfast tray, to reduce the waste when realized that not all passengers use the provided jam in their tray. The airlines bonus scheme offer crew the opportunity to earn bonuses of up to 50% of their salary depending on how profitable the company by the end of fiscal year. Singapore Airlines total cost, less fuel, labor, depreciation, and aircraft rentals is, at 29.1%, lower than other large airlines' average of 38.2%.

In Summary, Singapore Airlines is a world-class airline that serves a market niche in the aviation industry, maintains a high-end client-tell, and reputation for world class services. Singapore Airlines maintain profitability through constant cost cutting approach in conjunction with their world-class crew that significantly contributes to the airlines success and business strategy implementation.

References

2. Wirtz, J., & Heracleous, L. (2016). Singapore Airlines: Managing Human Resources for Costeffective Service Excellence. In *SERVICES MARKETING: People Technology Strategy* (pp. 695-703).

3. Airlines, S. (2016). Our Awards.

4. Lim, K. Y. (2017). *An exploratory mixed methods analysis of the media framing of crisis stakeholder salience: The case of Singapore Airlines SQ006* (Doctoral dissertation, Institute of Lifelong Learning).

5. Zentner, A. (2016). Service as a Strategy: A Review of Singapore Airlines. *Browser Download This Paper*.

6. Zentner, A. (2016). Service as a Strategy: A Review of Singapore Airlines. *Browser Download This Paper*.

7. Deshpande, R., & Lau, D. H. (2016). Singapore Airlines: Premium Goes Multi-Brand. *Harvard Business School, Case Study*, (9-517), 017.

8. Lawton, T. C. (2017). *Cleared for take-off: structure and strategy in the low fare airline business*. Routledge.

9. Heracleous, L., & Wirtz, J. (2014). Singapore Airlines: Achieving sustainable advantage through mastering paradox. *The Journal of Applied Behavioral Science*, *50*(2), 150-170.

10. Taneja, N. K. (2017). *Simpli-Flying: optimizing the airline business model*. Routledge.

11. Halpern, N. (2018). Airport business strategy. *The Routledge Companion to Air Transport Management*, 154.

12. Zentner, A. (2016). Service as a Strategy: A Review of Singapore Airlines. *Browser Download This Paper*.

Walmart

Company Background

Walmart is the largest company in terms of revenues in the USA, and one of the largest companies worldwide. Walmart is relatively new retail force that managed to dominate the retail sector in the United States. Bigger than Europe's Carrefour, Metro AG, and Tesco combined, Walmart the world's number one retailer with some 2.2 million employees. In the US, Walmart operates more than 5,160 stores, including about 4,400 Walmart stores and 650 Sam's Club warehouses, and a growing number of smaller format stores. The company's faster growing international division (28% of sales) numbers more than 6,100 locations; Walmart is the No.1 retailer in Canada and Mexico and has operations in Asia (where it owns a 95% stake in Japanese retailer SEIYU), Africa, Europe, and Latin America.

Business Model

For long time Walmart maintained its image as leader in retail segment globally by leading on price and assortment. Walmart known for its EDLC (everyday low cost) and EDLP (everyday low prices). Walmart tends to impose its business model to the world by offering globally standardized products at low prices. This strategy helped the company to become the world's largest company. Walmart's business model is "Lead on Price" which gives the company leadership position. "Always Low Prices" is commonly known slogan of Walmart.

They're able to implement this business model by having one of the largest supply chains in the world. Walmart spent over $365 billion to purchase merchandise for its stores in fiscal year 2015. This gives the company immense bargaining power with its suppliers. And they have chance to reduce the cost with suppliers and get good price compare to other stores. This enables them to compete with competitors in price. Walmart uses cross-docking. In this strategy, inbound shipments from suppliers are unloaded directly into outbound trailers at distribution centres. Walmart own very effective distribution centres and it is one of the largest in the world. Walmart logistics has a fleet of 6,500 tractors, 55,000 trailers, and more than 7,000 drivers. These innovative strategies are helping Walmart succeed on pricing front.

Competitive Advantage

Referring to Porter's Five Forces Model, being the largest retailer in the world, Walmart's position is strong overall. Rivalry among its competitors is fairly weak. The threat of substitute products is also weak. Walmart exerts a great deal of effort in making sure they are innovative and meeting customer demands. The bargaining power of suppliers is weak as well. For most producers and suppliers Walmart would be their big client. Likewise, the bargaining power of buyers is also weak. There is a broad base of customers and a significant demand for low prices. Finally, the threat of new entrants is weak. Walmart has a scale of operation that is so great, it would take years, maybe even decades, for a new company to be on the same level. Even prominent companies today would have an extremely difficult time matching the costs and prices Walmart provide.

All above is possible because the company's value chain. Walmart's supply chain management is extremely cost effective. Another cost-effective method in Walmart's supply chain management is their ability to track the movement of products through the entire value chain. The company has good system to check whether the product is in shipment, in distribution centres inventory, in-store inventory or on the shelf, or at the cash register.

Another competitive strategy that they acquire is their distribution strategies. This also helped Walmart achieve low prices. Walmart's strategy is to plot stores outside of large cities and within 200 miles of existing stores. Clustering stores together in small areas, Walmart relies on word-of-mouth advertising to win over consumers in larger cities. Because stores are close together, distribution costs are below average. Furthermore, Walmart seeks to meet different customers' needs with four distinct retail options; these include discount stores, supercenters, Sam's Clubs, and neighborhood markets. Each store concept has a specific range of store size, total employment, and estimated sales.

Another competitive strategy that makes Walmart efficient is, the company spends much less on advertising than does their competition. This is because of their clustering of stores in a relatively small area. Because their stores tend

113

to be grouped together so this enable them to spread advertising expenses across a single market and cut on advertising costs. All these activities include the technology used in tracking product (operations and distribution), relationships with suppliers, have proven to be successful overall as Walmart earned $256 billion in revenues and $9 billion in profits in 2004.

Business Strategy

The business strategy "always low prices" made through years but, many customers from highly concentrated population areas may think Walmart as a mass retailer with low price, low quality and prefer buy in other specialized stores. For long time, Walmart maintained its global leadership in retail segment by leading on price and assortment. Walmart's legendry EDLC (everyday low cost) and EDLP (everyday low prices) and this have make it become the world's largest company.

Developments in the retail environments and the evolving consumer preferences have forced Walmart to improve its business model and include two new strategies. They understand low costs strategy at all costs mixed with a growth strategy one again at all costs is not for a long run.

This is because their business model has limitation where it will not promise customer loyalty. In this model of 'low costs' philosophy, if people can find cheaper elsewhere they will leave for sure.

For example, if one of Walmart stores is badly located, or too far from another supermarket, where even the prices in the nearest competing supermarket are slightly higher, people will impartially tend to go to the nearest shop. There is no loyalty in retaining customers here. For this Walmart innovate upon its business model and include two new strategic levers. Walmart business now is led by the following four strategic pillars, which are; lead on price, invest to differentiate, be competitive on assortments, and deliver a great experience.

Another issue here is that Walmart tend to impose their business model by offering globally standardized products at low prices. This strategy has proven to be globally fatal as in the case of Walmart, Korea, Walmart Japan, and other places around the world. This strategy also failed in Germany whereas in China it works well. Expansion strategy seems to fail for Walmart as their business model cannot be established in continental Europe because of the numerous regulations, competition by rival European retailors, and consumer behavior. Europeans do business differently, their mentality, their culture and habits are quite different from that of the US consumer.

In Germany for example, Walmart tried to enter the market and grow through acquisitions. Rapidly, it turned out that the beliefs, motivation and convictions of both parts were totally different from the managers' point of view. For instance, sharing hotel rooms in order to reduce costs was unacceptable by German managers. As well shoppers were not eager to be educated to follow American habits. They are used to small and more compact stores. So Walmart must adapt efficient expansion strategy according to various specific tastes, behaviors, cultures and customs according to customers in various countries or regions in order achieve successful expansion. Implementing this business model without any changes is simply impossible for continental European countries.

Going Forward
Walmart is now cutting back on store investments and spending more on electronic commerce by developing their website and driving more sales through their web and

116

downloadable application. Walmart is also planning to make some changes in its stores. According to the CEO, Doug McMillon, the company constantly recognizes situational changes and responds accordingly. *"Every store I go into has room to improve,"* McMillon said. He and Walmart U.S. CEO Greg Foran, outlined three main strategies for improving the business. McMillon cited empty shelves and slow checkout counters as two major and the company is working on improving its inventory efficiency and it's planning to open more checkout counters than ever before during peak shopping hours and holiday days.

References

Muñoz, C. B., Kenny, B., & Stecher, A. (Eds.). (2018). *Walmart in the Global South: Workplace Culture, Labor Politics, and Supply Chains*. University of Texas Press.

Taillie, L. S., Ng, S. W., & Popkin, B. M. (2016). Walmart and Other Food Retail Chains. *American journal of preventive medicine, 50*(2), 171-179.

Pippert, T., & Zimmer Schneider, R. (2018). "Have You Been to Walmart?" Gender and Perceptions of Safety in North Dakota Boomtowns. *The Sociological Quarterly, 59*(2), 234-249.

Barney, J. B. (2012). Purchasing, supply chain management and sustained competitive advantage: The relevance of resource-based theory. *Journal of supply chain management, 48*(2), 3-6.

Noe, R. A., Hollenbeck, J. R., Gerhart, B., & Wright, P. M. (2003). *Gaining a competitive advantage*. Irwin: McGraw-Hill.

Casadesus-Masanell, R., & Ricart, J. E. (2010). From strategy to business models and onto tactics. *Long range planning, 43*(2-3), 195-215.

Richardson, J. (2008). The business model: an integrative framework for strategy execution. *Strategic change, 17*(5-6), 133-144.

Thompson, A., Peteraf, M., Gamble, J., Strickland III, A. J., & Jain, A. K. (2008). *Crafting & Executing Strategy 19/e: The Quest for Competitive Advantage: Concepts and Cases*. McGraw-Hill Education.

Chuang, M. L., Donegan, J. J., Ganon, M. W., & Wei, K. (2011). Walmart and Carrefour experiences in China: resolving the structural paradox. *Cross Cultural Management: An International Journal, 18*(4), 443-463.

Brea-Solís, H., Casadesus-Masanell, R., & Grifell-Tatjé, E. (2015). Business model evaluation: quantifying Walmart's sources of advantage. *Strategic Entrepreneurship Journal, 9*(1), 12-33.

Firend, A. R. (2009). Mergers & Acquisitions lessons from the Asian financial crisis. *Wealthmatrix, 11*(1), 100-103.

Laszlo, C., & Cescau, P. (2017). *Sustainable value: How the world's leading companies are doing well by doing good*. Routledge.

Akter, S., Wamba, S. F., Gunasekaran, A., Dubey, R., & Childe, S. J. (2016). How to improve firm performance using big data analytics capability and business strategy alignment?. *International Journal of Production Economics, 182*, 113-131.

Casadesus-Masanell, R., & Heilbron, J. (2015). The business model: Nature and benefits. In *Business models and modelling* (pp. 3-30). Emerald Group Publishing Limited.

Dyer, J. H., Godfrey, P., Jensen, R., & Bryce, D. (2015). *Strategic Management: Concepts and Cases*. Wiley Global Education.

SAMSUNG ELECTRONICS

Background

Samsung is a South Korean company founded in 1938. The word Samsung in Korean means "three stars" was founded by Byung-Chull Lee in 1938 with about 25 US dollars. Trade export was the business focus initially, selling Korean fish, fruits and vegetables two Chinese traders. Fast forward 10 years, Samsung started their own flour mills confectionery machines, manufacturing, sales operations, and as such, grow to become the modern global corporation that still bears the same name today. Samsung Electronics is part of Samsung Group, which is the largest semiconductor manufacturers in South Korea and the worlds. Samsung manufacturer consumer goods, including digital TVs, cell phones, cameras, computers, monitors, LCD panels and variety of other related products and services. Semiconductors products range from DRAMs, flash memory, display drivers; and communications devices. Most of Samsung are initiated in Asia and distributed does the rest of the world. By 2014, the total number employees at Samsung reached 489,000 globally, asserting dominance in number of industrial and consumer products.

The Business Model

Samsung Electronics is operating in different market segments such as consumer electronics (visual display, digital appliances, printing solution, health & medical equipment), IT & mobile communications (mobile communication, network, digital imaging) and device solution (memory, system LSI, LED business) capitalizing on cheap Korean labor. In the post North– South Korean war of the 1950's, S. Korea was wiped out. The U.S. assisted S. Korea by transferring of technology to take advantage of cheap labor. Initially, South-Korean products was suffering from lack of quality. It was no match to the popular Japanese products, which started to invade global markets slowly largely because good quality and low-cost. However, Korean manufacturers including Samsung, went through the learning curve slowly, taking advantage of the Japanese manufacturing experience.

However, most of Korean production was consumed by the US and European markets. By the mid-90s, the quality of Korean products begun to improve significantly. Such improvement in quality and low value of the Korean currency, assisted Korean companies to expand globally rapidly. The advantage that Samsung was able to capitalize on is the combination of cost competitiveness and advancements technological processes, including transfer of technology and joint venture operations with Japanese manufacturers.

SAMSUNG BUSINESS MODEL CANVAS

KEY RESOURCES	VALUE CREATION	CUSTOMER CHANNEL
•Hardware Products •Employees •Management	•Brand •Innovation •SCM and SIX SIGMA	•Distributers
		CUSTOMER RELATIONSHIP •Personal Assistance: After sale service
KEY ACTIVITIES •Manufacturing •Research and Development •Investing in startups	**VALUE PROPOSITION** •Cutting Edge Technology •GREAT DESIGN •Cheap Prices •Green Products	**CUSTOMER SEGMENT** •MASS MARKET •Corporate Buyers

COST STRUCTURE	REVENUE
•Manufacturing Cost •Research and Development cost •Distribution cost •Marketing and Advertisement cost	•Selling Products •Information and Communication Services •Financial Services

Business Model Analysis (Part 1) – Samsung Corporation. Source:
http://www.samsung.com/us/aboutsamsung/

Challenges

With the global slow economic growth and China's slowing demand, Samsung is focusing on identifying growth engines, developing innovative technology and pursuing creative solution. This strategy seems to be paying off as revenues are growing throughout 2015 and 2016. Strong financial management, strengthening global presence, and capitalizing on brand value is positioning Samsung as a leader and strong competitor across their industries.

Samsung commitment to lead innovations in technology stems from their motto "Inspired the World, Create the Future". Samsung is currently investing their resources to design and provide new value to their customers while improving share value of their employees and stakeholders. More Importantly, Samsung Electronics is well aware that future growth is dependent on the exploration and innovation in new business areas such as healthcare and biotechnology. Maintaining competitive advantage across all industries is dependent on improvements to their business model and constant innovation especially in the post Galaxy S7 cell phone fiasco that left an indent to the name of Samsung.

References

Moon, H. C., & Lee, D. (2004). The competitiveness of multinational firms: A case study of Samsung Electronics and Sony. *Journal of International and Area Studies*, 1-21.

Michell, T. (2010). *Samsung Electronics: And the Struggle For Leadership of the Electronics Industry*. John Wiley & Sons.

Leachman, R. C., Kang, J., & Lin, V. (2002). SLIM: Short cycle time and low inventory in manufacturing at Samsung Electronics. *Interfaces*, *32*(1), 61-77.
Yu, S. (1998). The growth pattern of Samsung electronics: A strategy perspective. *International Studies of Management & Organization*, *28*(4), 57-72.

Kim, C. E., Lee, K. H., Choi, J. W., & Yoo, J. S. (2010, July). The study of building a learning organization and cross-evaluation between companies applied DLOQ: Focusing on Samsung electronics f team practices. In *Computers and Industrial Engineering (CIE), 2010 40th International Conference on* (pp. 1-6). IEEE.

Borrus, M., Ernst, D., & Haggard, S. (Eds.). (2003). *International production networks in Asia: rivalry or riches*. Routledge.

Baloh, P., Uthicke, K., & Moon, G. (2008). A business process-oriented method of KM solution design: A case study of Samsung Electronics. *International Journal of Information Management*, *28*(5), 433-437.
Kim, Y. (1997). Technological capabilities and Samsung Electronics' international production network in Asia.

Pitkethly, R. H. (2001). Intellectual property strategy in Japanese and UK companies: patent licensing decisions and learning opportunities. *Research Policy*, *30*(3), 425-442.

Hemmert, M. (2014). The business system of Korea. *Asian Business and Management: Theory, Practice and Perspectives, 2nd edn. Basingstoke, UK: Palgrave Macmillan*, 219-238.

TOYOTA MOTORS

Company Background

Toyota Motor Corporation was founded in Japan by Kiichiro Toyoda in 1937. Over the years, Toyota has become the world's largest automaker with surpassing America's General Motors in 2008. Toyota sales of vehicles have been consistently increasing over the years. For instance, sales has increased from 6 million in 2003 to more than 10 million vehicles in 2014 across 170 countries. Their annual income is more than US$ 8.2 billion, which is larger than the combined income of its two main competitors, General Motor (GM) and Ford, and their net profit margins is 8.3 times higher than the average of their industry. The word Toyota is synonymous with the word quality, an image that resonates in global consumer's mind along with efficiency, reliability and economy.

Business Model

Toyota's success is attributed to its consistent improvements and innovation, which made it as one of the world greatest automotive makers. For instance, Toyota Production System (TPS) developed internally, which is an integrated socio-technical production system, developed to encompass their management philosophy and practices. TPS consists of 14 principles, which is employee focused, customer centric, open communication, innovative culture, leadership, prioritization, and just-in-time lean production.

Toyota success of TPS attempts to consider other essential factors such as culture and communication. Toyota combines the aspects of hard innovation and corporate culture as soft culture. Toyota sees employee as a valuable asset for growth of their company as it believes that the system alone is not sufficient to lead to any success. Along with best practices such as the Toyota Production System, Toyota heavily invests in developing their employees' capabilities.

Employees are constantly required to brainstorm to overcome challenge with great ideas. As employees grapple with challenges, efficient and effective solutions are generated from understanding different aspects of a given problem. Toyota employees are willing and encouraged to come up with new innovative ideas The cross-corporate innovative culture, and TPS is one of the reasons that puts Toyota forward, which has been overlooked by many rivals in the past. Toyota constantly attempts to improve their processes to be in line with fast changing global demand and technological innovation. However, many industry analysts have accused Toyota as a company that moves slowly. For instance, Toyota took 4 years to open its first plant in Kentucky after its joint venture with GM (New United Motor Manufacturing) in Fremont, California although Toyota was capable of moving forward faster than that, yet as per the Japanese cultural norms, the attempt to make changes requires time and daunting negotiations. Toyota adopts both; differentiation and low-cost production strategic approach to provide customers with a variety of choices according customer's demand. **Toyota has become a cost leader in the market, by adopting lean production, careful choice of models, control of suppliers, efficient distribution, and low service cost because of the high quality of their products.**

Toyota adopts proactive strategic orientation to keep its market position strong. It tries to produce new automobile every year with the new idea to be in line with new technological changes and markets orientation. Toyota was the first automobile corporate to launch a hybrid engine to be incorporated with an internal combustion engine, which is an environmental friendly approach and looking to introduce fully electric model in the near future. Toyota position itself to be at the front of their rivals and take advantage of opportunities such as weakness and vulnerability in competing car designs. Toyota senior executives constantly reinforce the message *"There's a better way"*. The motto of former Toyota chairman, Watanabe, *"No change is bad."* From this point of view, Toyota is a constantly growing company.

Toyota adopted an organizational management style that benefits them the most. Most top management are Japanese men, who has been at the company for a very long time and promised a life-time job in return for their loyalty and hard-work. Toyota is still located at their original location "Mikawa" in rural Yamagata area, northern Tokyo. Employees' salaries are paid at a special discounted rate, which is much lower than market rate. Toyota's top executives earned about 1/10 less than that of Ford executives. However, employees choose to stay at Toyota largely because of their sense of belongingness, which is a culture created by Toyota company.

To save cost at Toyota, employees switch off all lights during lunchtime, and usually work together in a larger room to reduce space utilized and renting expense. At the same time, Toyota spends large amount of money on manufacturing facilities, dealer networks, and human resource development. For example, Toyota spent $22 billion in production and supporting facilities and more than $170 million was spent annually in competing Formula One circuit over the past 6 years. This makes Toyota's management system as very efficient management system.

The unwritten Toyota rule internally as far as communications is concerned, is that everything must be keep simple and short in both formal and informal communications. For example, the summarized information, analysis, action plan and expected results are expected to be in a single page during presentations. However, in terms of social network, Toyota encourages their complex web to let everybody knows what goes on at the company. Flat communication style among employees across functional and geographic boundaries, and grouping them according to specialization and year of entry, created vertical relationships for teaching and mentoring. Fostering informal ties by inviting employees to join activity clubs according to their interests and hobbies provide a sense of belonging and a healthy internal organizational environment.

Toyota's goals are purposely set high in order to foster creativity, improve quality, and forcing different functional areas to collaborate across the rigid silos in which they usually operate. The former chairman of Toyota, Watanabe, said that his goal is to *"build a car that makes the air cleaner, prevents accidents, makes people healthier and happier when they drive it, and gets you from coast to coast on one tank of gas"* (Lessons from Toyota's Long Drive, HBR July–August 2007). Toyota allows their employees to make mistakes and learn from failures. One of the cornerstones of Toyota's philosophy is "you don't need to have a great plan to start; you can try and continuously improve step by step". By this mean, Toyota encourages its employees to step out of their comfort zones.

Toyota provides its employees with a set of Standard Operating Procedures (SOP) as a guide to strictly follow. Based on such SOP, employees are geared to improve gradually and constantly on their effective and efficient manufacturing and production capabilities. The status quo of employee is challenged by the (8 step TBP layout). The 8 steps process is designed to clarify the problem; break down the problem; set a target; analyze the root cause; develop countermeasures; see countermeasures through; monitor both results and processes; and standardize successful processes. The A3 report, named for a sheet of paper 11 inches by 17 inches, is another SOP communication tool. By this means, Toyota forces employees to capture essential information needed to resolve a given problem in a single sheet that they can widely disseminate across the organization.

Open communication is another core value of Toyota in creating failure tolerant culture. As Toyota expanded into numerous countries around the globe, its operations has expanded significantly, which caused the quality of internal communications to deteriorate. As a result, it has become difficult to coordinate operations across markets and product groups. However, Toyota managed to stabilize company's expansion and growth by forcing sharing of same corporate values among employees across the globe, working toward common goals, ensuring open communications, and effective people management. Toyota's success is largely attributed to its management style. Such style is aligned with cultural values of management and employees, which has proven to be an asset for the company. Toyota's corporate strategy stems from their constant improvement efforts across the organization (the Japanese concept of "Kaizen" which is constant and long-term improvements) and their sense of innovation in meeting global demands. Such process of constant improvements allowed Toyota to start with simple cars, reliable and economic cars, to evolve as one of the world top automakers as they celebrate their 75 years anniversary.

References

Kusuda, Y. (2008). Toyota's violin-playing robot. *Industrial Robot: An International Journal, 35*(6), 504-506.

Liker, J. K., & Franz, J. K. (2011). *The Toyota way to continuous improvement: Linking strategy and operational excellence to achieve superior performance* (Vol. 1). New York: McGraw-Hill.

Noe, R. A., Hollenbeck, J. R., Gerhart, B., & Wright, P. M. (2003). *Gaining a competitive advantage.* Irwin: McGraw-Hill.

Cusumano, M. A. (2010). *Staying power: Six enduring principles for managing strategy and innovation in an uncertain world (lessons from Microsoft, Apple, Intel, Google, Toyota and more)*. Oxford University Press.

Aaker, D. A. (2006). Brand portfolio strategy. *Strategic direction, 22*(10).

Imai, M. (2012). *Gemba Kaizen: A commonsense approach to a continuous improvement strategy*. New York: McGraw Hill.

Stevenson, W. J., & Hojati, M. (2007). *Operations management* (Vol. 8). Boston: McGraw-Hill/Irwin.

Dussauge, P., Garrette, B., & Prahalad, C. K. (1999). *Cooperative strategy: Competing successfully through strategic*

Hamel, G., & Prahalad, C. K. (1993). Strategy as stretch and leverage. *Harvard business review, 71*(2), 75-84.

Peng, M. W. (2002). Towards an institution-based view of business strategy. *Asia Pacific Journal of Management, 19*(2-3), 251-267.

Gupta, Y. P., & Somers, T. M. (1996). Business strategy, manufacturing flexibility, and organizational performance relationships: a path analysis approach. *Production and Operations Management, 5*(3), 204-233.

Beiker, S. A. (2015). Evolution–Revolution–Transformation: A Business Strategy Analysis of the Automated Driving Industry. In *Road Vehicle Automation 2* (pp. 139-151). Springer, Cham.

Zokaei, K., Lovins, H., Wood, A., & Hines, P. (2016). *Creating a lean and green business system: techniques for improving profits and sustainability*. Productivity Press.

Mourdoukoutas, P. (2015). *Business strategy in a semiglobal economy*. Routledge.

Harmon, P. (2015). The scope and evolution of business process management. In *Handbook on business process management 1* (pp. 37-80). Springer, Berlin, Heidelberg.

Sisson, J., & Elshennawy, A. (2015). Achieving success with Lean: An analysis of key factors in Lean transformation at Toyota and beyond. *International Journal of Lean six sigma, 6*(3), 263-280.

Hunter, P. (2016). *The Seven Inconvenient Truths of Business Strategy*. Routledge.

132

TATA Motors

Company Background

TATA Motors of India, formerly known as TELCO (short for (TATA Engineering and Locomotive Company) is an Indian multinational automotive manufacturing company headquartered in Mumbai, Maharashtra, India and a subsidiary of the TATA Group. Its products include passenger cars, trucks, vans, coaches, buses, construction equipment and military vehicles. It is the world's 17th-largest motor vehicle manufacturing company, fourth-largest truck manufacturer, and second-largest bus manufacturer by volume[3].

TATA Motors has auto manufacturing division and assembly plants in Jamshedpur, Pantnagar, Lucknow, Sanand, Dharwad, and Pune in India, in addition to Argentina, South Africa, Thailand, and the United Kingdom. TATA has research and development centers in

Pune, Jamshedpur, Lucknow, and Dharwad, India and in South Korea, Spain, and the United Kingdom. TATA Motors' principal subsidiaries purchased the British premium car-maker Jaguar Land Rover (the maker of Jaguar, Land Rover, and Range Rover cars) and the South Korean commercial vehicle manufacturer TATA Daewoo. TATA Motors has a bus-manufacturing joint venture with Marcopolo S.A. (TATA Marcopolo) is a construction-equipment manufacturing joint venture with Hitachi (TATA Hitachi Construction Machinery), and a joint venture with FiatChrysler, which manufactures automotive components and FiatChrysler and TATA branded vehicles.

Founded in 1945 as a manufacturer of locomotives, the company manufactured its first commercial vehicle in 1954 in collaboration with Daimler-Benz AG, which ended in 1969. TATA Motors entered the passenger vehicle market in 1991 with the launch of the TATA Sierra, becoming the first Indian manufacturer to achieve the capability of developing a competitive indigenous automobile[4].In 1998, TATA launched the first fully indigenous Indian passenger car, the "Indica", and in 2008 launched the TATA Nano, the world's cheapest car. TATA Motors acquired the South Korean truck manufacturer Daewoo Commercial Vehicles

Company in 2004 and purchased Jaguar Land Rover from Ford in 2008.

TATA Motors is listed on the Bombay Stock Exchange, where it is a constituent of the BSE SENSEX index, the National Stock Exchange of India, and the New York Stock Exchange. TATA Motors is ranked 287th in the 2014 Fortune Global 500 ranking of the world's biggest corporations

Business Model

TATA Motors business model is to manufacture low cost vehicles to provide them with a greater scope of earning high profit margins and enjoys a greater market share. Economic slowdown has increased the competition to provide quality and low priced vehicles. With good understanding of rural culture, Indian economy and incomes of the farmers, TATA Motors increased its concentration in providing commercial and passenger vehicles market with winning products in the compact, mid-size car and utility vehicle segments (Thakkar 2010). What contributes to the success of their business model, TATA Motors successfully applies a 'Low-Cost Strategy' by providing unmatched value for its customer's money. 50 years of experience in automotive industry enabled the company to served varied needs of its customers by providing many range of products. TATA Motors is a pioneer in R&D as well. This allowed them to be constantly innovative and improve on existing technologies.

Their business model was too obvious when they were listed in Guinness Book of World Records for manufacturing world's cheapest car TATA Nano. TATA Nano received global media attention because of the low price, and delivery to customers started in mid 2009, with a starting price of 100,000 Rs, which is approximately UK£ 1,360 or US$ 2,171 (as of October 2009). Making it the cheapest car in the market, affordable to low incomes families and individual.

TATA is to expand its business in the Indian car market by 65%. The question is, how could TATA structure their business model in such a way to provide low cost vehicles. TATA reconstructed the manufacturing process breaking down every component of the car into its smallest pieces eliminating everything that is absolutely unnecessary and outsourced its manufacturing to a limited number of suppliers. The number of parts have been reduced with changes such as one windscreen wiper instead of two, no power steering, three lug nuts on the wheel instead of four, no tubes in the tires, only one side mirror and the basic version has no air conditioning, no power windows, no fabric seats, radio or central locking and the seats are fixed except for the driver's which is adjustable.

The fascinating part of Nano is constructed in such a way that can be built and shipped separately to be assembled in a variety of locations around India. It was sold in kits, assembled, distributed, and serviced by local businesses in rural areas, adjusting the car for local needs, adding value in the process to the product and receiving replacements for broken cars. All this while the car actually meets all Indian emission, pollution, and safety standards.

As for the business model, TATA motors strived to be a low cost leader in the automobile market. The company understands the fact that this only possible through low cost strategy. The most evident example is that of the ultra-low cost Nano. To effectively execute such business model, they excessively invested in R&D to ensure innovations that can add value to the product at minimum cost. This included designing sophisticated eye-catching models.

They also adopted sustainable practices and maintain healthy relations with all the members of the value chain and constantly upgrade their knowledge.

Competitive Advantage

One advantage of TATA Motors is their constant advances in automobile technology through heavy research and development. They employ approximately 1,400 scientists in the R&D function. TATA Motors has several research and development centers in India. According to the company, the research center in Pune was amongst the finest in the country. They host forums to develop and test durability, engine performance, emission, safety, design and style, noise, hydraulics, tracks, and instrumentation. TATA company is currently focusing on equipping vehicles of the future with improved communication, navigation and entertainment technology.

Such concept car, is a fiberglass vehicle that virtually powered by air and is emission free, weighing only 350 kg powered by piston engine that runs on compressed air. This model is to run between 200 to 300 kilometers on one Euro of compressed air. According to *Moteur Development International*, the proposed model's engine is efficient, cost-effective, scalable, and capable of other applications, such as power generation this would make it a flagship of the next generation green vehicle.

Choosing strategic locations is of additional advantage to TATA Motors. TATA is located in India, a developing country with abundance of human and natural resources offered at extremely low prices. As such, location plays a vital role in TATA's success. TATA advantage of manufacturing in India allows labor cost at only 8 to 9% of cost of sale, compared to 30 to 35% of cost of sale in developed countries. Moreover, India is one of the world's largest producers of automotive components. This provides TATA Motors with direct access to many parts and components. This provides TATA with competitive advantage and more bargaining power with suppliers since they are the largest car manufacturer in the country.

High levels of demand caused by improvements in infrastructure and population growth, enabled TATA to take full advantage of the Indian automotive market. According to Society of Indian Automobile Manufacturers *"India is a place where 1.4 million new cars are sold each year this being a huge attractive market for TATA*

Motors". Additionally, the India government introduced protective regulations that are very favorable to TATA. All factors described above, combined together, they form the bases for TATA's successful business model that allows it to compete in one of the world most competitive industries and grow to buy rival companies.

References

1- Johnson, M. W., Christensen, C. M., & Kagermann, H. (2008). Reinventing your business model. *Harvard business review*, *86*(12), 57-68.
2- Gamble, J. E., Thompson, A. A., & Peteraf, M. A. (2013). *Essentials of strategic management: The quest for competitive advantage*. McGraw-Hill/Irwin.
3- Hayes, R. (2006). Operations, strategy, and technology: pursuing the competitive edge. *Strategic Direction*, *22*(9).
4- Li, C. (2010). Groundswell. Winning in a world transformed by social technologies. *Strategic Direction*, *26*(8).
5- Palepu, K., Anand, B. N., & Tahilyani, R. (2011). Tata Nano-The People's Car.
6- by Sara Carter, E., & Jones-Evans, D. (2009). Enterprise and small business: Principles, practice and policy. *Strategic Direction*, *25*(5).
7- Becker-Ritterspach, F., & Bruche, G. (2012). Capability creation and internationalization with business group embeddedness–the case of Tata Motors in passenger cars. *European Management Journal*, *30*(3), 232-247.
8- Anderson, J., & Markides, C. (2007). Strategic innovation at the base of the pyramid. *MIT Sloan management review*, *49*(1), 83.
9- Grant, R. M. (2016). *Contemporary strategy analysis: Text and cases edition*. John Wiley & Sons.
10- Becker-Ritterspach, F., & Bruche, G. (2012). Capability creation and internationalization with business group embeddedness–the case of Tata Motors in passenger cars. *European Management Journal*, *30*(3), 232-247.
11- Lim, C., Han, S., & Ito, H. (2013). Capability building through innovation for unserved lower end mega markets. *Technovation*, *33*(12), 391-404.
12- TATA company website: www.tata.com

13- *Moteur Development International: https://www.mdi.lu/*
14- Society of Indian Automobile Manufacturers:
http://www.siamindia.com/

KIA Motors

Company Background

KIA Motors was founded on 11th December 1944, and is the oldest car company in South Korea. Initially, they started as a steel company and manufacturing parts and bicycles. Today, they are South Korea's second largest automobile manufacturer with headquarters in Seoul. Initially, KIA was a manufacturer of steel tubing and bicycle parts by hand and operated as one of Korea's *Chaebols* (a business group consisting of large companies that are owned or managed by relatives and family-owned conglomerates)[2]. By 2017, KIA's sales grew to $6.2 billion USD[5].

Business Model:

As Korea's second largest manufacturer and one of the main players in the international automobile market, KIA produces more than 1.4million cars a year. KIA has a total of 14 manufacturing and assembly operations in eight other countries. To ensure post-sale service, sold vehicles are serviced through a wide network of more than 3000 dealers and distributors in 172 countries. Today, KIA employs over 40,000 people and reports over US$17 billion in annual revenues.[3]

In South Korea, KIA mainly operates in three major vehicle assembly plants. They are; Hwasung, Sohari and Kwangju facilities. Outside Korea, KIA has numerous manufacturer and assembly plants. KIA has a long history of building locally to meet the specific needs of local customers, with assembly operations using "car kits" (supplied from Korea) in Ecuador, Iran, Malaysia, Russia, and Vietnam.[3] In Slovakia, KIA has completed their first-ever European engine and vehicle assembly plant. Now, they own and operate a manufacturing facility in China. KIA also penetrating in West Point, USA as of late 2009. Overall, these new manufacturing plants not only have the capacity to build up to 300,000 vehicles annually, but provides flexible assembly lines that can manufacture different models at one time in order to adapt to global changes in buying trends.

As far as research and development (R&D) is concerned, KIA has 8000 technicians at Namyang, which is a world-class research and development center with designers and experts from the USA, Europe, Japan and other countries. These experts have worked for other leading automotive brands in their countries, and now serving KIA to put them on the lead of auto manufacturers. KIA also formed an Eco-Technology Research Institute near to Seoul. The institute is working on hydrogen fuel-cell vehicles for the future as well as state-of-the-art end-of-life vehicles recycling technologies and processes[3]. Essentially, Kia spends 6% of the company revenues on research and development. In addition to having local research and development plans, KIA also runs research centers in USA, Japan and Germany. To achieve KIA ambitions to be one of the worlds' premier automotive brand, consumer's preferences are KIA's main concern. Therefore, KIA has been investing in new headquarters in both Europe (Germany) and USA to be close to their consumer base and better understand trends and changing in their largest market segments.[3]

Problem and solutions

However, there are always unpredictable events in the global markets, or an unforeseen consequences. Left with little options, KIA declared bankruptcy in 1997 during the

Asian financial crisis. The following year in 1998, Hyundai Motor Company acquired 51% share of KIA, it outbid Ford Motor Company which has owned an interest in KIA Motors since 1986. Moreover, after some subsequent divestments, Hyundai Motor company price share dropped to less than 50%. Yet, they remained as KIA largest stakeholder.[2]

Continuous effort by KIA to recover from financial crisis was on going. KIA's strategy was to focus more on the global market. In 2005, KIA decided to increase sales in the European market, by focusing their attention on European consumers. By hiring Peter Schreyer as Chief Designer Officer (CDO) in 2006, KIA was able to create a new corporate culture.[2] The new corporate team culture, new designs and new approach to serving European consumers helped KIA to expand their sales in Europe. A new investment of US$1 billion in manufacturing facilities in Georgia, West Point, during October 2006 allowed KIA to win the 15th consecutive year of increasing their US market share.

Strategies

KIA has a long-term plan and determination to achieve growing share of the international markets, to achieve this,

KIA has appointed a German car designer, Peter Schreyer as the chief design officer. At the same time, KIA is investing in two design centers in Germany and USA, which hire young multi-national teams of designers to improve their designs. This stems from KIA's conviction that design will allow them to continue to expand their global market share, and therefore, improving design and quality will significantly contribute to the increase of market share and the KIA brand name. KIA has a long-term plans and determination to achieve growth in their global market share. To this end, KIA has appointed a German car designer, Peter Schreyer as the Chief Design Officer (CDO). At the same time, KIA is investing in two design centres in Germany and USA, that hires young multi-national teams of designers to improve overall designs and introduce new concepts. This stems from KIA's conviction that design will allow them to continue to expand their global market share, and therefore, improving design and quality will significantly contribute to increase market share and the brand name.

To succeed in European market, KIA was able to put more creative efforts to differ themselves from other brands. KIA look into what matters most to consumers. KIA realized that warranty is of a primary concern to consumers. As a result, KIA offered a seven years after sales warranty on their vehicles. This warranty duration was way longer than the standard two years warranty commonly offered by other brand in Europe. KIA's actions to place their attention on vehicle's quality gained them much respect better ratings and consumer attraction to their cars. KIA awareness that the people inside the vehicle are the focal point from consumer's stand point, they improved the quality of materials used in cars interior, brought to their cars a driver oriented premium elements such as; innovative comfort features, modern audio systems, individual interior variants and workmanship are examples of interior quality improvements. All vehicles built had to be inspected by specialist according to the highest product standards in the automobile industry was another essential element of the strategic mix of KIA. KIA was aware that they had to diversify designs to effectively compete in a very competitive global automotive market. As such, they were innovative with their brands by designing new KIA petrol and diesel engines, which incorporated numerous technological advancements that reduces fuel consumption and improved fuel to mile efficiency. Additional actions were taken to minimise operational cost, delivering

147

improved dynamics, durability and enhanced drivability experience to the consumer.[4]

Results:

In 2015, KIA came in 74th place on *Interbrand's* ranking as 100 "Best Global Brands" with estimated brand value of US$57 billion. KIA's position in the ranking has been on the rise ever since, to be ranked as the 69th best brand by 2017.[4] In the coming years, KIA plans to continue their investment in research and development to develop a full-line-up of vehicles across all segments. KIA further their efforts to improve their concept of cars, by providing a better experience and transportation solutions to consumers world-wide.[3]

References

1. *International Directory of Company Histories, Vol. 29. St. James Press, 1999.* Retrieved 2015, from http://www.fundinguniverse.com/company-histories/kia-motors-corporation-history/
2. Retrieved 12 Dec 2015, from https://en.wikipedia.org/wiki/Kia_Motors
3. COPYRIGHT (C) 2015 KIA MOTORS CORP. Retrieved 2015, from http://www.kia.com/eu/company/kia-motors-corporation/
4. COPYRIGHT (C) 2015 KIA MOTORS CORP. Retrieved 2015, from http://www.kia.com/eu/quality/
5. COPYRIGHT (C) 2015 KIA MOTORS CORP. Retrieved 2017, from http://pr.kia.com/en/main.do
6. COPYRIGHT (C) 2015 KIA MOTORS CORP. Retrieved 2015, from http://pr.kia.com/en/company/ir/financial-information/financial-highlights.do

7. Kim, J. J., & Do, S. H. (2008). Recent development and applications of magnesium alloys in the Hyundai and Kia Motors Corporation. *Materials transactions*, *49*(5), 894-897.

8. Barron, A., Pereda, A., & Stacey, S. (2017). Exploring the performance of government affairs subsidiaries: A study of organisation design and the social capital of European government affairs managers at Toyota Motor Europe and Hyundai Motor Company in Brussels. *Journal of World Business*, *52*(2), 184-196.

9. Machková, H., & Collin, P. M. (2015). Market entry strategies of passenger carmakers-The case study of the Czech Republic. *Central European Business Review*, *4*(3).

10. Bloomfield, G. T. (2017). The world automotive industry in transition. In *Restructuring the global automobile industry* (pp. 19-60). Routledge.

11. Bohnsack, R., Pinkse, J., & Kolk, A. (2014). Business models for sustainable technologies: Exploring business model evolution in the case of electric vehicles. *Research Policy*, *43*(2), 284-300.

12. Jain, H., & Kaushik, S. (2018). Making of Two South Korean Chaebols: Samsung and Hyundai. *International Journal of Advance Research, Ideas and Innovations in Technology*, *4*(1), 173-176.

ASUSTEK COMPUTER

Company Background

ASUS of Taiwan takes its name from Pegasus, the winged horse in Greek mythology that symbolizes wisdom and knowledge. ASUS was founded in Taipei, Taiwan in 1989 by four people who had previously worked at Acer as hardware engineers, T. H. Tung, Ted Hsu, Wayne Hsieh and M.T. Liao.[1]

ASUS would describe their humble beginnings by creating a prototype for a motherboard using Intel 486, but it had to do so without access to the actual processor. ASUS pride itself for being able to solve Intel's motherboard problem by making ASUS' own motherboard, which works appropriately without the need for further modification. Since then, ASUS was receiving Intel engineering samples ahead of its competitors. [1][2]

150

However, economic slowdown caused a decreasing number of potential clients, which significantly affected their business on both, the long-term and short-term. As such, ASUS invested considerable time and effort to come up with optimal business model to maintain operations profitability and growth. [5] Today, ASUS, is ranked as the world's top 3 consumer notebook vendors and the maker of best motherboard manufacturer in the world, which has been voted as the world's "Best Motherboard Brand" for six consecutive years by readers of Tom's Hardware Guide (THG). [4][6]

Business Model

Taiwan as a country has grown into information technology hub and a dominant player in the global technology market. ASUS was able to create a competitive advantage among motherboard manufacturers with a handful of employees. ASUS winning formula was marketing with quality, speed to market, innovation, service and maintaining competitive cost. As such, every employee was asked to master the *"ASUS Way of Total Quality Management"* to deliver on its promise of *"Persistent Perfection"*. [4]

ASUS widely attributed with reforming the PC industry with world class R&D team of 3,000 engineers. ASUS innovativeness earned them many world's firsts, such as the introduction of the ground-breaking Eee PC™, the ingenious use of renewable materials like leather and bamboo in notebooks and the power saving Super Hybrid Engine technology into its notebooks and motherboards and reduces temperatures inside the PC.[4] Relying on their creativity, ASUS managed to gain an advantage over others suppliers. ASUS's appetite for technological innovation, investments in R&D, focusing on quality products and services, and maintaining long-term relationships with customers allowed them to carve a name in their industry and grow profitably.[4]

ASUS ability to continuously improve their quality management practices, control processes, maintain customer's satisfaction as priority, and focusing on creating cost advantage, ensured long-term relationships with clients and brand loyalty. ASUS employees are key to their success. Employees share common purpose with the company and strive for innovativeness and quality. They take the challenges of competing in new era very personal.

ASUS have set up mandatory training classes on design. [8]

The design thinking process has seven stages: define, research, ideate, prototype, choose, implement, and learn. These seven steps, helps employees formulate problems by asking the right questions and formulate creative solutions. The ZenFone 2 smartphone is a good example of design thinking process. According to research firm BCN, ASUS successfully topped into Japan's smartphone market with a 29.6 percent market share in the first half of 2015 [9].

Today, ASUS is considered to be a significant player in cloud computing as they focus on developing products according to changing market need and changing consumer trends.

Reference:

1- http://www.asus.com/us/About_ASUS/Brand_Promise/
2- ASUS Company Information < By Mast Business. Mastbusiness.com. 3 January 2008. Retrieved 8 December 2015.
3- http://www.asus.com/us/About_ASUS/The_Meaning_of_A SUS
4- http://www.asus.com/us/About_ASUS/Winning_formula/
5- http://www.wikiwealth.com/swot-threat:asus:bad-economy
6- http://www.asus.com/us/About_ASUS/Marks_in_History_ ASUS_Motherboards/
7- https://en.wikipedia.org/wiki/Cloud_computing
8- http://www.engadget.com/2015/08/16/asus-chairman-jonney-shih-interview/
9- https://en.wikipedia.org/wiki/Design_thinking

10- Michael, D., Kappos, D. J., & Villasenor, J. (2015). Models of Intellectual Property Collaborations Between Mature and Emerging Market Companies. *MIT Sloan Management Review, 56*(4), 12.

11- Kuo, T. K., Lim, S. S., & Sonko, L. K. (2018). Catch-up strategy of latecomer firms in Asia: a case study of innovation ambidexterity in PC industry. *Technology Analysis & Strategic Management*, 1-15.

12- Cortez, M. A. A., Ikram, M. I. M., Nguyen, T. T., & Pravini, W. P. (2015). Innovation and financial performance of electronics companies: A cross-country comparison. *Journal of International Business Research, 14*(1), 166.

BAIDU

Company Background

Baidu is China's premier and most important search engine. Founded in 2000 the company was established by Robin Li & Eric Xu, China natives who studied and worked in the United States[6]. As of 2015, Baidu is ranks as the 4th in Alexa Internet rankings[7]. Prior to founding Baidu, Mr. Li worked for IDD Information Services, a division under Dow Jones and Company[6]. There, he patented a technology to his name, which came very handy late on when forming Baidu search engine[6]. Since then, Baidu has expanded its business, offering a wide variety of internet based services that range from search engines to a community of encyclopedia similar to that of Wikipedia[6].

Business Model

Early on, when Baidu was just a startup, they licensed their searching services to bigger web sites and charged them per each search[3,6]. As the cost grew overtime for clients, some decided to delay payments, as such, relationships began to sour between them. And therefore, Baidu was forced to develop their own website. As they grow, and in attempt to improve revenue streams, Baidu began to welcome advertisers and invite them to post their adverts on Baidu search engines. Google is a main competitor with serious ambitions to rival Baidu in the Chinese market, started to finance Baidu for future acquisition. This would most defiantly provide Google, a cash rich company with long-term advantages as far as China is concerned. However, the relationship didn't take off well between the executives of the two companies. When Baidu decided to go public, multiple offers poured in from Cash rich companies such as SoftBank, Yahoo, Microsoft and Google. However, going public provided the needed funds to expand operations and dominate the search engine market in China, while making Mr. Li, China's first Web billionaire[6] with the ability to utilize his wealth to invest in other technology and Internet based companies.

Thanks to close collaboration, support and compliance with government regulations, Baidu managed to drive off Google entirely from the Chinese market. Strategically, it is very good move to eliminate a fierce competitor and allowing them to corner the search engine market. There are however complaints by some that Baidu plays unfairly by penalizing whoever supports their competitors, by influencing their search results. Accusations also included the fact that advertisers, who chose to reduce how much they pay Baidu, were also affected by Baidu's search results. Baidu's CEO strongly rejected such accusations and describing them as merely "conspiracy theories". With such tight regulations imposed by the government on Internet search companies, the CEO is respectful of the law of the land understands well that compliance will allow him to stay in business. He views himself as an entrepreneur, and therefore he must wisely navigate through various obstacles and regulations to maintain creditability and secure future market share.

This in turn, will only give him a competitive advantage in China. The Chinese government does not see it self as close to Baidu as many people think. In fact, the Chinese government released numerous news and documentaries about Baidu's practices that affected the company's reputation in many ways. The Chinese government went one step further by hiring a company to develop a new search engine all together, and by which, sending a strong message to Baidu that they should not think that they have monopoly over search engines in China.

This of course, made Baidu more motivated to be more creative, innovative, competitive and to diversify their investments. This also puts more pressure on Baidu to maintain good relationship with the government.

Baidu's competitive advantage is found in many places. Their initial support by the government most defiantly gave them initial advantage, their U.S. trained CEO with good experience and patented technology is an asset to the future of the company. The collection of people who work at Baidu are also considered to be among the best in China with very creative abilities.

In the early days before Google was driven out of the market, Google seriously wanted to compete with Baidu. However, Baidu was able to convince the Chinese market that it knew China better when compared with Google. This was done through commercials and targeted advertisements campaigns[6].

Foreign competition is not the only concern for Baidu, they have to worry about rising competitive giants within the Chinese market such as Alibaba and Tencent. To e ahead of the game, Baidu began its expansion into the Brazilian market during 2014, by launching a Brazilian search engine and acquiring a local e-commerce web site[4,5].

Baidu's CEO made it clear through his recent announcements in 2017 that the company plans to expand into multiple IT related sectors and capitalizing on the Baidu name and financial power by bringing the Baidu brand to more countries around the world.

References

1. Baidu: Registrar 'incredibly' changed our e-mail for hacker. (n.d.). Retrieved November 28, 2015, from http://www.computerworld.com/article/2520068/security0/baidu--registrar--incredibly--changed-our-e-mail-for-hacker.html
3. Barboza, D. (2010, January 13). Baidu's Gain from Departure Could Be China's Loss. Retrieved November 28, 2015, from http://www.nytimes.com/2010/01/14/technology/companies/14baidu.html?_r=0
4. China web giant Baidu launches search engine in Brazil. (2014, July 18). Retrieved November 28, 2015, from https://www.techinasia.com/baidu-launches-search-engine-in-brazil/
5. China's Baidu buys control of Brazil's Peixe Urbano in expansion push. (2014, October 9). Retrieved November 28, 2015, from http://www.reuters.com/article/2014/10/09/us-peixe-urbano-m-a-baidu-idUSKCN0HY1EN20141009
6. How Baidu Won China. (n.d.). Retrieved November 28, 2015, from http://www.bloomberg.com/bw/magazine/content/10_47/b4204060242597.htm
7. Top Sites. (n.d.). Retrieved November 28, 2015, from http://www.alexa.com/topsites/global

8. Jia, K., & Kenney, M. (2016). *Mobile Internet Business Models in China: Vertical Hierarchies, Horizontal Conglomerates, or Business Groups*. BRIE Working Paper 2016-6.

9. Deans, P. C. (2015). Teaching social business strategy from a global perspective. In *Paper presented at the SIGED: IAIM Conference*. AIS Electronic Library (AISeL).

10. Choi, B. (2017). Corporate Strategy of Baidu, Alibaba, Tencent for Electric Vehicle (EV) Business. 중국과 중국학, (31), 219-250.

11. Holopainen, M. (2017). Business model innovation to manage dominant design A case study at Tele2 and Comviq.

12. Linz, C., Müller-Stewens, G., & Zimmermann, A. (2017). *Radical Business Model Transformation: Gaining the Competitive Edge in a Disruptive World*. Kogan Page Publishers.

13. Greeven, M. J., & Wei, W. (2017). *Business Ecosystems in China: Alibaba and Competing Baidu, Tencent, Xiaomi and Leeco*. Routledge.

IKEA

Company Background

Based in Southern Sweden, IKEA is the largest retail furniture company in the world, with global revenue of 36.3 billion Euros by the end of 2017. Founded by Ingvar Kamprad in 1943, the name Ikea is formed from the founder's initials (I.K.) plus the letters of Elmtaryd (E) and Agunnaryd (A), the farm and village where he grew up. IKEA humble beginnings was selling pens, wallets, picture frames, table runners, jewellery and nylon stockings. By 1948, Kamprad added furniture to his product line, and in 1949, he published his first catalogue.

Business Model

Today, IKEA has grown into a global brand with 127,000 workers in 41 countries. IKEA offers home furnishings and accessories of trendy and practical design while being functional at a low price. Affordability and appeal to the masses is of primary focus of Ikea then and today.

IKEA visitors are surpassing 590 million annually across the globe. In addition to the visitors in the stores, some 450 million visitors are tracked visiting IKEA's website. IKEA's main marketing channel is still its catalogue that is distributed globally with 191 million copies, in 56 different editions and 27 different languages displaying some of IKEA's 9500 different products.

IKEA's business model is to offer a wide range of modern designs, functional furnishing products, decent quality and affordability at low prices. IKEA uses inexpensive materials in a new way, by which minimizing production process, distribution and retail costs to maintain low prices. IKEA's philosophy is based on consistency in consumer expectation.

As per the words of IKEA director *"We began learning about the production of furniture 60 years ago. We had just begun to design our own furniture and needed to learn how best to match the possibilities of the supplier with the needs of the customer. Bringing the two closer together was how we would keep prices low. Since then we've continued to apply these methods and to work with supplier's right on the factory floor. What we today call democratic design influences and benefits every part of IKEA - from our development facilities in Älmhult, to our suppliers around the globe, including local artisans in places like India and South East Asia"* (IKEA home pages).

In 2000, IKEA launched IWAY, their supplier code of conduct. All home furnishing suppliers must comply with IWAY requirements, otherwise they are phased out (IKEA Home Pages-People & Communities). The IWAY Standard helps in the process of positive developments. It outlines IKEA's minimum requirements concerning the environment, social impact, and working conditions.

IKEA monitors the implementation of IWAY by regularly visiting their suppliers to check and ensure compliance and implementation of IWAY Standards. IKEA reports that there are about 80 auditors and independent third party auditors that go around making both announced and unannounced visits, checking on suppliers and their sub-suppliers.

The IWAY Standard requirements includes; no child labor, no forced or bonded labor, no discrimination, freedom of association, at least minimum wages and overtime compensation, safe and healthy work environment, and preventing pollution to air, ground and water and work to reduce energy consumption (IKEA Home Pages-People & Communities).

References

1. Background of IKEA. Available from: http://www.scribd.com/doc/59951004/Case-Analysis-IKEA#scribd
2. The IKEA Business Model. Available from: Supplierportal.ikea.com/doingbusinesswithIKEA/Documents/The%20Business%20Model.pdf
3. About IKEA. Available from: http://www.staffs.ac.uk/schools/business/resits/postgrad/InternationalSupplyChainMgmtIKEACaseStudy.pdf
4. The Economist - The secret of IKEA's success (24th Feb 2011) Available from: http://www.economist.com/node/18229400
5. IKEA. Available from: http://www.ikea.com/ms/en_AU/about-the-ikea-group/company-information/
6. Insider Business - Retail. Available from: http://www.ft.com/cms/s/0/83389238-5819-11e3-82fc-00144feabdc0.html
7. USA Today - IKEA Want To Get A Little More Personal, 14 June 2015 Available from: http://www.usatoday.com/story/money/2015/06/12/ikea-30th-anniversary-us-expansion/71066656/
8. Grant, R. M. (2016). *Contemporary strategy analysis: Text and cases edition*. John Wiley & Sons.
9. Waage, S., & Anderson, R. (2017). Integrating sustainability into business strategy and operations: applying The Natural Step approach and Framework and backcasting from principles of sustainability. In *Ants, Galileo, and Gandhi* (pp. 61-80). Routledge.
10. Mendibil, K., Rudberg, M., Baines, T., & Errasti, A. (2016). Operations Strategy and Deployment.

11. Pham, T., Pham, D. K., & Pham, A. (2016). *From Business Strategy to Information Technology Roadmap: a practical guide for executives and board members*. CRC press.
12. Håkansson, H., & Snehota, I. (Eds.). (2017). *No Business is an Island: Making Sense of the Interactive Business World*. Emerald Publishing Limited.
13. Gassmann, O., Frankenberger, K., & Csik, M. (2016). Innovation Strategy: From new Products to Business Model Innovation. In *Business Innovation: Das St. Galler Modell* (pp. 81-104). Springer Gabler, Wiesbaden.
14. DaSilva, C. M., & Trkman, P. (2014). Business model: What it is and what it is not. *Long range planning, 47*(6), 379-389.

TENCENT

Tencent 腾讯

Company Background

Based in Shenzhen, China, Tencent is the largest Internet company in China. Tencent develops and provides entertainment, media, and online advertising across China[1]. Some of their most popular products and services includes websites and communication platforms such as QQ.com, WeChat, JD.com and League of Legends. In April 13th 2015 the company was valued at US$206 billion[2]. On September 8 of 2015, they surpassed Alibaba Group's share value[3].

Challenges

Many industry analysts and competitors' claims that Tencent is unauthentic copycats, and has no innovation[4]. Some even go as far as describing Mr. Huateng Ma, chairman of Tencent as the 'copycat king'. Mr. Ma replied to such accusations by saying "Copying is not evil". In fact,

166

Tencent is viewed from a strategic point of view to be very successful largely because of their copycat approach they have been pursuing[6]. To dismiss such accusations, Tencent applied for 1,086 patents in 2014 to the World Intellectual Property Office (WIPO)[5]. Early on in the beginning of the company, they imitated AOL's ICQ messenger and named it "OICQ"[7]. To avoid the potential threat of a lawsuit from AOL, they renamed the program to "QQ", which means cute in chinese[7].

Business Model

The current Tencent business model can be divided into three sectors, which are value added services, online advertising and other businesses[8]. Value added services provide fee-based revenue from social networks and online games. As of 2014, this sector contributed more than 70% of Tencent's revenue[8]. These are mostly VIP monthly subscription for an array of social media and video game services that Tencent offers.

Online advertising gives traffic-based revenue mainly from brand advertising and performance advertising[8]. Brand advertising capitalizes on the reach from QQ.com and its own video streaming site much like YouTube and provides advertising services on those platforms for clients. Social performance advertising is targeted advertising similar to that of Facebook. Users will only see advertising targeted to their habits and usage patterns on social media platforms. An additional component of their business model is integrated online payment services, which provides transaction based revenue[8]. Brands under this category are Weixin Payment, QQ Wallet and TenPay. The combination of these three brands, provides Tencent a combined base of over 200 million accounts linked to bank cards. This makes Tencent the number 2 online payment platform in China[8].

The Future

Realising that its own country is the next emerging market aimed by the whole world, Tencent decided to offer its huge network of services and users to selected chosen companies for future profitable partnerships. On January 2015, they expanded their agreement with the National Basketball Association (NBA) to enhance NBA's presence in China[9]. The deal gives Tencent the exclusive digital partner of the NBA in China, which boosts advertising revenue for Tencent.

Around the end of 2014, Tencent made an agreement with Sony Music Entertainment to distribute and promote artists under the Sony label like Daft Punk and Bob Dylan[10]. They also partnered with Warner Music Group to bring artists like Bruno Mars and Red Hot Chili Peppers to China legally[11]. Jointly with Fox International Channels, Tencent will be providing 300 hours of National Geographic content to the Chinese market[12]. They will also coproduce original content aimed specifically at the China viewers.

Anticipated future moves include partnership with 20th Century Fox Film Corp[13]. Such partnership mainly targets to tap into the vast social network of QQ, selling movie themed virtual items like emoticons to its users and at the while promoting titles that belong to 20th Century Fox. Partnering with YG Entertainment tapping into artists such as "Psy", "Big Bang" and "2NE1"[14]. This is largely because of the rising popularity of Korean cultural wave of pop music in China. The partnership will facilitate China's access to YG music and music video content, utilising Tencent's platforms. In November 2015, HBO attempted to expand into China by choosing Tencent as its business partner[15]. This partnership will give China access to HBO TV dramas and movies through Tencent Video platform, and subject to various Chinese government approvals. This is an effort to legally provide customers with original content in a market flourishing with piracy. Such arrangement is advantageous move for Tencent, since a main competitor like Alibaba has already partnered with "Lions Gate" to increase their own access and variety of content. With such strategic partnership formed by Tencent, it reflects China's position as enormous consumption ability and demand level for media content, which will play dominant role in this century. This further shows that while Tencent has an enormous structure of profitable networks, it endlessly requires content and intellectual property to be conveyed through such networks to keep up with increasing consumer demand and competitive landscape. This could partly explain the unleashing of creativity and innovation in the media sector in the face of changing industry and the emergence of new players such as Netflex, Amazone and others, where content and access to markets are primary component for gaining competitive advantage.

References

1 Biographical Dictionary of New Chinese Entrepreneurs and Business Leaders, Pg. 111-112 Ilan Alon and Wenxian Zhang. Edward Elgar Publishing, 2009. Google Book Search.

2 China's Tencent hits $200 billion market cap for first time". http://www.reuters.com/article/2015/04/13/us-tencent-valuation-idUSKBN0N40WN20150413

3 Chen, Lulu Yilun (8 September 2015). "Alibaba $141 Billion Slide Boosts Tencent to Asia's Biggest". *Bloomberg Business*. Retrieved 9 September2015.

4 Tencent's innovation is copied... Machine translation xinhuanet.com, April 13, 2007

5 Nearly two-thirds of the world's patent applications come from three countries. (n.d.). Retrieved December 6, 2015, from http://qz.com/365448/nearly-two-thirds-of-the-worlds-patent-applications-come-from-three-countries/6 http://www.chinese-champions.com/tencent-technology/

7Jucha, Nicolas (2012-09-01). "QQ – China's instant messenger". gbtimes. Retrieved 2012-04-14.

8 Tencent Investor Presentation. (2015). Retrieved December 6, 2015, from http://www.tencent.com/zh-cn/content/ir/fs/attachments/InvestorPresentation.pdf

9 Eben Novy-Williams (30 January 2015). "NBA Expands China Business With Five-Year Tencent Extension". *Bloomberg.com*. Retrieved 14 August 2015.

10 Tencent, Sony strike China music distribution deal. (2014, December 16). Retrieved December 6, 2015, from http://www.reuters.com/article/us-tencent-sony-music-idUSKBN0JU0UN20141216#wO9KpiIc2vUIUUe8.97

11 Warner Music, Tencent in China Distribution Deal. (n.d.). Retrieved December 6, 2015, from http://www.wsj.com/articles/warner-music-tencent-in-china-distribution-deal-141586922212 http://tbivision.com/news/2014/12/fox-strikes-nat-geo-deal-chinas-tencent/369581/

13 Tencent, 20th Century Fox form reel venture. (n.d.). Retrieved December 6, 2015, from http://www.chinadailyasia.com/business/2015-12/05/content_15354628.html

14 China's Tencent Pacts With South Korea's YG Entertainment. (n.d.). Retrieved December 6, 2015, from http://www.hollywoodreporter.com/news/chinas-tencent-pacts-south-koreas-753205

15 Tencent to Distribute HBO Dramas, Movies Online in China. (n.d.). Retrieved December 6, 2015, from http://www.wsj.com/articles/tencent partners-with-hbo-to-distribute-tv-dramas-movies-online-in-china 1416902891

16 Jia, K., Kenney, M., & Seppälä, T. (2017). *Supercell Joins a Mobile Internet Giant: Fitting into Tencent's Overall Business Strategy* (No. 54). The Research Institute of the Finnish Economy.

17 Jia, K., Kenney, M., Mattila, J., & Seppala, T. (2018). The Application of Artificial Intelligence at Chinese Digital Platform Giants: Baidu, Alibaba and Tencent.

18 Greeven, M. J., & Wei, W. (2017). *Business Ecosystems in China: Alibaba and Competing Baidu, Tencent, Xiaomi and Leeco*. Routledge.
19 Bereznoi, A. (2015). Business model innovation in corporate competitive strategy. *Problems of economic transition, 57*(8), 14-33.

BMW: Active-E "DriveNow"

The Business Model

Although BMW is a well established around with reputation for high-quality German engineering yet the company understand very well the changing nature of the industry and the ever harder environmental standards and declining sales. As such, BMW is adapting to the new reality of their industry.

Faced with changes in technology that it's making it possible for consumer to switch to electric car for instance, poses numerous threats to the company. For example, companies such as Google and Apple among others are venturing into fully mobile electric car. This is a clear indication of the changing mechanism in an industry that is traditionally dominated by the elite few with two German manufacturers actors on the top of the chain, which are Mercedes and BMW (Nelson January 5, 2015).

The point here is the viability of the business model and the inevitable change that must happen to all existing businesses models. The BMW "DriveNow", which will be discussed here is under testing phase in the city of San Francisco where other players such as Apple electric car and Google electric cars are being tested as well. "DriveNow" is fully electric car with the concept of car sharing rather than car ownership that is being pioneered by BMW. The value lies in the ability of the driver to just drop the car at any location without worrying about parking space and able to get back to it any time while charging its batteries in an easy to find location through an application when needed.

Fundamentals of the Business Model

The value proposition is: such service is proposed to cost $39.32 USD per minute, or $90 per day. Thus, the concept of ownership will be eliminated and opens the door towards multiple transportation methods to get to a destination in an ever-congested cities. This is a workable concept especially in big cities where people are constantly on the move and prone to high efficiency, Time conscious and no desire to own a car.

For this model to work, number of element must be effectively managed, such as the development of the application, getting customers input regarding the activities and desire towards such a service and most importantly for me multiple partnerships with key service providers for this model to work (Appendix-I). According to (Nelson January 5, 2015) BMW obtained an investment from BMW's own group (i Ventures) venture capital firm to assist in financing 70 Active-E cars and 8 "DriveNow" power electric stations. The service designed as a location-based mobility type of service.

Key elements of the Business Model;

Declining sales in big cities worldwide with the exception of China is a clear indication to BMW that there is a fundamental shift in the automotive industry (Tobin 17 October 2014), which needs to be taken into account. Therefore, BMW is attempting to capitalize on mobility in transportation rather than ownership.

The testing of "DriveNow" is an attempt by BMW to validate the concept and reaffirm the evolution and their business model. Big aspect of the validation of the evolving business model is creation of value to the consumer by testing the concept as whole, which is not limited to testing the new business model in transportation, but rather, testing the actual creation of value that is ultimately the bedrock of the new business model (Tobin 17 October 2014). BMW is well aware of their limitation at the initial stages of the introduction of Active- E car, and hence, attempts to include as many partners to make the new business more effective and workable.

The Future

It is clearly that BMW is capitalizing on the future of transportation here with the "DriveNow" concept. Utilizing their eventual capital arm "iVenture" was all available resources where BMW to validate the feasibility of the new concept, something which is their main competitors in the automotive industry and outside it, attempting to do this, reflects a clear realization by the giants in the industry and technology companies that shift in industry characteristics poses an opportunity and creates a new landscape. Those who do not take advantage of shifting realities, are bound to be left behind. In conclusion, BMW will continue to be a major player in the transportation business and in the automotive industry for years to come, capitalizing on their history of fine engineering, market share, image, reputation and consumers' expectations.

References

1- BLOOMBERG, FEBRUARY 24, 2017. *LUCID MOTORS AIMS TO RIVAL TESLA*

2- Bergen, M. 24 February 2017. *Ambitious Engineer at Center of Colossal Fight Between Google and Uber.* Bloomberg

3- Dana Hull and David Welch. *Tesla Is Burning Through Cash,* Bloomberg Technology. 23 February 2017

4- Nelson, G. January 5, 2015. *How BMW cracked the streets of San Francisco,* Automotive News

5- Tobin, D. 17 October 2014. *BMW brings car sharing to UK with DriveNow scheme,* The Sunday Times

6- Turrentine, T., & Garas, D. (2015). Regional Trends in Electromobility-Regional Study North America.

7- Santini, D. J., & Zhou, Y. (2015). Potential to electrify miles with different plug-in vehicle innovation paths. In *Transportation Research Board 94th Annual Meeting.*

LONPAC INSURANCE

LONPAC INSURANCE

Company Background

Lonpac Insurance is a Malaysian company. It is the wholly owned subsidiary of LPI Capital Bhd. that was formally known as London & Pacific Insurance Company Bhd[1]. Lonpac currently has more than 21 branches in Malaysia and an international branch in Singapore. Lonpac's business model plays a vital role in Lonpac's success.

Business Model

Lonpac provides its customers a variety of products. Mainly property insurance, liability insurance, pecuniary insurance, employees benefits insurance, project insurance, motor insurance and marine insurance. Lonpac also provides customer with packaged personal insurance products, designed for individual financial protection against a variety of unexpected misfortunes. This includes

---

[1] Lonpac's Official Website, n.d

travel insurance, care plus, privilege car protector and others.

Lonpac provides customers with valued services. One of which is the Lonpac E-Assist for its comprehensive private car insurance policyholders. Lonpac E-Assist provides 24 hours a day emergency towing services, minor roadside repairs, car rental referral services and arrangement for hotel accommodation in the event of a car breakdown or accidents. Lonpac also provides Home-Assist, which is a complimentary referral assistance programme to all Lonpac's House owner and Householder policyholders.

Lonpac Home-Assist helpline connects to the right help when clients faces inconveniences. It includes electrical assistance, plumbing assistance, locksmith assistance, leaking roof, pest control, air-conditioning services and cleaning and restoration of carpets. Clients are happy that Lonpac could provide them with such comprehensive solution.

Corporate clienteles are usually the ones that contribute the most to Lonpac's revenues. This is because they usually sign up for more than one class of insurance and are having a few policies in each class. With the wide range of high profile clients, Lonpacs distribution channels come mainly from agents who earn their commission by finding new customers. Each agent is only allowed to have two general insurance principals and one life insurance principal.

The marketing department is usually the ones that work together with these agents where they communicate and receive applications from agents and have them processed by underwriting department, before issuing the policy. International clients are handled by a specialized global department. Public Bank recommends clients to Lonpac or it may be a requirement to take up Lonpac's insurance in order for a loan to be approved.

Allocated financial institution department handles these public bank accounts. Having strategic partners helps improve Lonpac competitive position in the marketplace. Lonpac partners consist mostly of international companies. Lonpac also acts as an intermediary insurance company that provides insurance to international organizations that have branches or subsidiaries and operates within Malaysia. Lonpac's success may also be attributed to its technical, support and business development division. In short, it lies with its employees' unique culture, given the way they operate, manage and work together, which defines their effectiveness and efficiency.

In the near future, Lonpac is expected to face challenges when the markets for fire and motor insurance will be facing de-tariffication where insurance companies can free to price their products. Over the years, both the fire and motor insurance have strictly followed the tariffs set by the central bank "Bank Negara". This will pose challenges because the insurance industry generally is facing intense local and international competition. Maintaining competitiveness will be based on the ability to provide the lowest insurance rate around. Lower rates however, would then mean a lower premium collected compared to the pre de-tariffed market. Lower premium would mean a sharp decline in revenues. Competition would also increase. Lonpac has yet to come up with a way to tackle this challenge.

Reference

1- Nourani, M., Devadason, E. S., Kweh, Q. L., & Lu, W. M. (2017). Business excellence: the managerial and value-creation efficiencies of the insurance companies. *Total Quality Management & Business Excellence*, 28(7-8), 879-896.

2- Nourani, M., Chandran, V. G. R., Kweh, Q. L., & Lu, W. M. (2018). Measuring Human, Physical and Structural Capital Efficiency Performance of Insurance Companies. *Social Indicators Research, 137*(1), 281-315.

3- Afroz, R., Akhtar, R., & Farhana, P. (2017). Willingness to Pay for Crop Insurance to Adapt Flood Risk by Malaysian Farmers: An Empirical Investigation of Kedah. *International Journal of Economics and Financial Issues, 7*(4).

4- Azizan, N. A., Kweh, Q. L., & Ting, W. K. I. (2015). Efficiency of Malaysian politically connected insurers: revisiting the resource-based view. *Journal for International Business and Entrepreneurship Development, 8*(3), 202-214.

5- Nawi, M. A. A., Ahmad, W. M. A. W., & Aleng, N. A. (2014, October). Efficiency of General Insurance in Malaysia Using Stochastic Frontier Analysis. In *STATISTIKA: Forum Teori dan Aplikasi Statistika* (Vol. 11, No. 2).

6- Wu, Y. C., Kweh, Q. L., Lu, W. M., & Azizan, N. A. (2016). The impacts of risk-management committee characteristics and prestige on efficiency. *Journal of the Operational Research Society, 67*(6), 813-829.

7- Wu, Y. C., Kweh, Q. L., Lu, W. M., & Azizan, N. A. (2016). The impacts of risk-management committee characteristics and prestige on efficiency. *Journal of the Operational Research Society, 67*(6), 813-829.

LEVI STRAUSS & CO.

Company Background

The history of Levis jeans goes back to 1853, as Levi Strauss & Co. is attributed to inventing denim blue jeans. With such history of success, the company has lost its competitive advantage in the era of hyper competition, fast changing consumer taste, and growth in global consumption of blue jeans that experienced a rise in the number of designer and manufacturers of such hot and fashionable product.

Business Model

Twenty years ago, Levi Strauss avenues were over $7 billion USD, which place them ahead of Nike. Levis was then the "Cool" jeans to own. However, over the past two decades, Levi had a self-imposed set of actions that caused the company to loose market share. Levis had developed a mounting debt over the years, made a bad decision regarding their wholesalers, when they treated wholesalers and retailers alike, which proved to be a mistake. Adding to Levis's problem, denim blue jeans also has its own fashion cycles, like most products.

However, over the past couple of years, Levi Strauss company has experienced a turn around. Levi Strauss went through an overhaul in their business strategy and re-inventing their business model. This started with new management of Levi Strauss that focused on re-shaping their marketing strategy and taking advantage of new wave in denim blue jeans fashion that proved to be a success for the company. The new Levi Strauss management team managed to reduce corporate debt, made some successful investments for the company, and grew beyond their traditional men blue jeans to improve their collective blue jeans offerings. Their introduction of women denim blue jeans included items such as "Levis back-wings tops", which sold over 4 million pieces globally in 2017, doubling their sales from the year before.

The back-wings tops are extremely popular in The U.S., Europe and amongst the Asian consumer, a market with over 2 billion potential consumers. Extending their product line beyond the traditional men blue jeans and their focus o new women fashion helped put them on top again. This is the result of their new marketing strategy, which is to take advantage of new cultural moment of hip consumers with lust for new and creative designs.

For instance, the pop-artist Beyonce made history wit her performance in early 2018 in Coachella, California, with millions of fans watching Beyonce performing wearing a Levis cut-off short jeans, without being paid or endorsed by Levis. Her performance and het cut-off Levis jeans spread like wildfire amongst her fans, and an entire generation of consumers' worldwide. Capitalizing of new designs, and abandoning sticking to one set of fashion, growing women fashionable designs and growing their online sales has lead to massive explosion in global sales, and a rebound in company's position as a leading blue jeans brand.

References
1- Levi Strauss & Co. corporate website:
   http://www.levistrauss.com/our-story/
2- The Economist, The meaning of blue jeans, March 26, 2016
3- Reiche, B. S., Stahl, G. K., Mendenhall, M. E., & Oddou, G. R. (Eds.). (2016). *Readings and cases in international human resource management*. Taylor & Francis.

4- Strauss, J., & Frost, R. D. (2016). *E-marketing: Instructor's Review Copy*. Routledge.

5- Dickson, M. A., & McCord, J. (2016). The integrated business strategy of a Central American denim apparel manufacturer. *Latin American Journal of Management for Sustainable Development, 3*(1), 66-79.

6- Lueg, R., Pedersen, M. M., & Clemmensen, S. N. (2015). The role of corporate sustainability in a low-cost business model–A case study in the Scandinavian fashion industry. *Business Strategy and the Environment, 24*(5), 344-359.

7- Burns, P. (2016). *Entrepreneurship and small business*. Palgrave Macmillan Limited.

8- Levi Strauss & Co. Celebrates 150th Anniversary. *PR Newswire* (Press release). May 1, 2003. Retrieved February 1, 2017.

SIME DARBY

Company Background

Official Known as Sime Darby Berhad, is a key Malaysia-based multinational conglomerate involved in 5 staple sectors: plantations, property, industrial, motors and energy & utilities. It was stablished in 1910, by two very different partners, William Middleton Sime was a 37-year-old Scottish explorer and Henry Darby was a rich 50-year-old English banker, owner of property in Northern Malaya. Together they ventured in the lucrative rubber plantation fields and later expanded to other fields like coca plantation, palm oil etc.

In the late 1970s, Sime Darby Holdings sold half of its equity to Malaysian investors, mainly through Tradewinds (Malaysia) Sendirian Berhad. In December 1979 with the merger of two new Malaysian bodies, Sime Darby moved its headquarters to Kuala Lumpur and became a Malaysian registered company. Although plantation sector remains the most important sector for the company, Sime Darby has spread out far locally and internationally involved in many types of businesses stretching from aerospace to tourism (Sime Darby, 2013).

Business Model

Initially Sime Darby encountered firm opposition from locals, who were distrustful of foreigners coming in to operate a plantation in Malacca. To repress their disapproval, Sime and Darby forged alliances with several members of the Chinese business community. The most prominent of those business leaders was Tun Tan Cheng Lock. Sime Darby made a fortune in the global rubber industry during the 1920s and 1930s. It purchased Sarawak Trading Company in 1929. Sarawak (later renamed Tractors Malaysia) uphold the franchise for Caterpillar heavy earthmoving equipment. That significant purchase gesticulated Sime Darby's expansion into the heavy equipment business, which would eventually become a major factor of its sprawling network.

Sime Darby's diversification proved to be a smart move. Demand for its oils and other agricultural products swelled during the late 1960s and 1970s, and the company began to accrue large profits. Through Consolidated Plantations, which was the company's main plantation subsidiary, Sime Darby became a leading strength in the region's booming agricultural sector. Alongside to growing the oil palms and cocoa, the company began processing the crops into manufactured products for deal worldwide.

Sime Darby discarded some of its poorly performing resources during the late 1970s and early 1980s. However, it also continued capitalizing in new ventures. By the early 1980s the company's drive to diversify had taken it in almost every industry, from agricultural and manufacturing to finance to health sector and real estate. It's diversify into heavy equipment, real estate, and insurance businesses, and modeling the new management also produced ample amounts of cash into the company's traditional commodity and plantation operations.

Sime Darby became a desired name of investors looking for a safe gamble. During the late 1980s and early 1990s much of Sime Darby's cash hoard into a mass of new companies and ventures. Sime became a relatively big actor in the global reinsurance business. Sime Darby earned a spectacular 65% average annual growth during the late 1980s and early 1990s. Despite its gains, critics charged that the company had focused too heavily on old-fashioned commodity industries and was unsuccessful to move into the 1990s with the rest of Malaysia.

Sime Darby began growing investments in businesses such as power generation, oil and gas, and exporting heavy equipment. After undertaking restructuring activities, Sime Darby managed to increase sales to US$3.15 billion in 1994, about US$186 million of which was stated as net income.

Under the mountains of success, Sime Darby does have its fair share of controversies. The company has been accused of violating the land rights of local communities in Liberia, holding a franchise for 220,000 hectares of farmland.

Local environmental and human rights groups have termed Sime Darby's contract with the Liberian government a "land grab," commenting that the contract does not justify for the ownership rights of the rural communities who live inside the designated area. In 2011, representatives field a formal complaint to the Roundtable on Sustainable Palm

Oil (RSPO), and in 2012 a group of communities signed onto a statement criticizing the contract. And in 2013, Sime Darby's name also held responsible of the fires on Indonesian plantations that caused widespread pollution issues in Malaysia and Singapore, many deaths, health issues and loss of homes. However, the company denied such allegations and their connection with the land clearing fire in Indonesia.

References

1- Huizingh, E. K. (2017). Moving the innovation horizon in Asia. *Technovation*, *60*, 43-44.

2- Foo, M., & Teng, P. (2017). Agriculture at the Crossroads: Bridging the Rural Urban Divide. *Food Security*, *9*(2), 401-404.

3- Mamun, M. A., Shaikh, J. M., & Easmin, R. (2017). Corporate Social Responsibility Disclosure in Malaysian Business. *Academy of Strategic Management Journal*.

4- Kadir, M. S. A., Sahallan, N. A., Ismail, M., Mazalan, M. I., & Sharif, S. (2016). THE FACTORS INFLUENCING RETIREMENT PLANNING MANAGEMENT (RPM) AMONG SIME DARBY RESEARCH EMPLOYEES: A CONCEPTUAL FRAMEWORK. *Journal of Business Innovation*, *1*(1), 1.

5- Basiruddin, R., Salam, Z. A., Isa, C. R., Rasid, S. Z. A., & Abidin, Z. Z. (2015). SLDU Palm Industries Sdn Bhd: The Blame Game In The Performance Measurement Systems. *International Journal of Innovation and Business Strategy*, *4*(2), 16-23.

6- Mohan, A. V. (2017). Human resource management and coordination for innovation activities: gleanings from Malaysian cases. *Asian Journal of Technology Innovation*, *25*(2), 246-267.

7- Mohan, A. V. (2017). Human resource management and coordination for innovation activities: gleanings from Malaysian cases. *Asian Journal of Technology Innovation*, *25*(2), 246-267.

8- Hussin, W., & Imani, W. N. (2017). Risk and performances: financial performance of sime darby berhad.

9- Chongvilaivan, A., & Menon, J. (2017). ASEAN'S OUTWARD FOREIGN DIRECT INVESTMENT. *Outward Foreign Direct Investment in ASEAN*, 30.

10- Mansor, M. F., Abu, N. H., Nasir, H., Kamil, S., & Missnon, M. K. A. (2015, August). The effect of cost reduction and business strategy on human resource outsourcing practicing: A study of Malaysian government link company. In *Technology Management and Emerging Technologies (ISTMET), 2015 International Symposium on* (pp. 238-242). IEEE.

GRAMEEN BANK

Grameen Bank

Grameen bank is a community-based independent microfinance institution. A Nobel Prize winner enterprise, founded by Dr. Muhammad Yunus in Bangladesh during 1983. The microfinance system has been commonly applied amongst people in numerous countries, but nowhere this idea has been successful and significantly contributing to the betterment of people's lives and reduced poverty level as in the case of Bangladesh. 94% of the total equity of the bank is owned by the public while the other 6% is owned by the Bangladesh government. The important factors that make Grameen Bank business model successful are; organizational structure, client centered delivery system, communication and culture.

Business Model

Grameen Bank was established to improve people's life's and contribute to rural development, both socially and economically by providing small loans. By giving loans as small as US $27 per family, the bank aims to give loan without collateral to the poorest of people in Bangladesh, which happens to be a majority of women. Microcredit, insurance, funds transfer and saving are examples of the different types of services provided through microfinance. The idea is successful because traditional banks will only provide financial facilities to people after a thorough check of credit history, owned assets and ability of repayment.

Since the poor segment of the population do not necessary meet such requirements, they are by default left out of the banking and lending system. And therefore, such segment of the population is left out of traditional banking and forced to borrow from small local lenders with high interest rates reaching up to 100%. Such high interest rates do not contribute to the betterment of people and found to cause even more financial problems in the long-run.

Grameen Bank is therefore looked at as distinct poverty mitigating institution. It is commonly known in

194

Bangladesh as bank of the poor. The 4 principles of Grameen bank are; discipline, courage, unity and hard-work. The credit and loans provided are designed to allow poor borrowers to invest in productive areas such as agriculture, livestock, processing and manufacturing, services and trade, forestry and fisheries. The bank primary emphasizes on assisting as many women as possible in rural areas. Such women is sought to be according to cultural norms as hard-working, reliable and significant segment of the population that makes a huge social and economic contribution to the nation. Grameen bank's main objectives remains as following;

- To expand banking services to the poor
- To eradicate money lenders' exploitation
- To utilize the manpower resources fully by creating self-employment opportunity to the disadvantaged
- To help the disadvantaged to understand their role in society and their socio-economic contribution.
- To turn around the circle of "low income, low savings, low investment, low income" into an extending system of "low income, credit, investment, more credit, more income"

The political angle to Grameen Bank intervention, is that such empowerment, tends to reduce the dependence on rural power elite. As such, when the poor are able to generate enough income, they do not need the economic support of the rich any longer. Moreover, since Grameen bank is an independent entity with minimum participation of state sponsored programs in rural development and the role of power elites in rural areas is ought to be minimized. It was noticed that as the poor become more aware of such opportunity and the possibility of economic independence, the exercise of voting rights have been practiced at a higher rate.

One of the main factors of Grameen Bank's success is organizational management, which is composed of two systems; delivery and receiving. The bank has its own delivery system, which consists of branch offices, area offices, zonal offices, and the head offices. These offices are organized in decentralized divisional structure with branch offices as profit centers. Officers are empowered with decision-making abilities and healthy internal communication is practiced as main component of the organizational culture. Top management will not interfere in the decision-making process at the field, while branch managers and area managers are to provide summarized reports annually according to their roles.

The branches and centers are the corner stones of the receiving end. A group of 5 like-minded economically disadvantaged people with no collateral are asked to form a group. The group members are then asked to choose someone they can trust as a leader, however, people from the same household or relatives are not allowed to be in the same group in order to avoid feud amongst family members. Moreover, groups are divided based on their gender as per local cultural norms.

In order to empower the borrowers with accountability, group members are asked to choose a chairperson and a secretary. Those positions will be rotated among the members on annual basis to encourage change and group development. Grameen bank workers liaise with chairpersons regarding issues related to loan utilization and discipline of group members through weekly meetings, whereby all members are expected participate on compulsory bases. This provides Grameen bank the transparency needed to communicate and nurture team spirit amongst members.

Grameen believes that through better communication, borrowers are more likely to return loans, as the bank is more aware of their problems. Borrowers as group members are fully educated about the Grameen rules, policies, responsibilities and social development activities before they are given the loans. Two members of a given group receives the loan first. If they show consistency in returning the loan through scheduled installments over 6-8 weeks, under group chairperson supervision, other 2 members will also receive their loans, while the chairperson receiving the loan lastly. Borrowers are allowed to invest the loan in area of their choice.

Loans tend to range from taka 3000 (US 75) to taka 10,000 (US 250) without any collateral. Instead of asking for assets collateral as in the case of traditional banks, Grameen bank uses social collateral. The loan must be repaid in 50 weekly installments, whereby borrowers are not eligible to have any other loan till they fully repay the initial loan. The first two members that received their loan first will be pressured by the other members to make payment on time. On the other hands, it is allowed for the group member to assist his/her members if they have genuine difficulty in repayment. If the entire group unable to settle the loan, only then the bank takes the risk on the loan. This approach by Grameen bank is believed to have increase customer's loyalty and popularity, encourages repayment, and achieves as of date an astonishing 98% return rate.

In term of human resource management, staffs are motivated through constant training programs. All the staffs are constantly being educated on the importance of their role and contribution to social and rural development. Emphases on hiring are focused on workload capacity, honesty, and sincerity. However, such high turnover rate comes with dissatisfaction by employees because of the highly demanding nature of operations in rural areas, which many new employees find it difficult to adapt to. In order to retain qualified staff with the necessary skills, Grameen Bank offers different types formal and informal rewards for both immediate and long-term results. Some rewards are recognition based, others include promotion, pride of performing a job that contribute to people's progress, bonus for being good team member, and providing sense of belonging to something larger than oneself. Grameen bank's success is built by the outstanding performance, committed, and motivated personnel.

In conclusion, providing a good solution to specific market segment, setting clear objectives, and strategies along with sense of contribution to the national socio-economic environments help in building one of the world most successful business stories. The story of Grameen bank is also a story of successful execution of unique business model and management by trusting both employee and customers. Winning employees through continuous improvements in their lives and the lives of customers while empowering and motivating employee to sustain customer loyalty have contributed to Grameen bank's success.

Reference

Sengupta, R., & Aubuchon, C. P. (2008). The microfinance revolution: An overview. *Federal Reserve Bank of St. Louis Review*, *90*(January/February 2008).

Zohir, S. (2004). NGO sector in Bangladesh: An overview. *Economic and Political Weekly*, 4109-4113.

Develtere, P., & Huybrechts, A. (2002). Evidence on the social and economic impact of Grameen Bank and BRAC on the poor in Bangladesh. *Research Paper. Hoger Instituut Voor De Arbeid. Katholieke Universiteit Leuven.*

Sarker, A. (2001). The secrets of success: The Grameen Bank experience in Bangladesh. *Labour and Management in Development, 2(1)*

Wahid, A. N., & Hasnat, B. (1993). *The Grameen Bank: Poverty Relief in Bangladesh*. Boulder, Colo.: Westview Press, c1993. xii, 305 p.: illustrations; 23 cm..

Papa, M. J., Auwal, M. A., & Singhal, A. (1995). Dialectic of control and emancipation in organizing for social change: A multitheoretic study of the Grameen Bank in Bangladesh. *Communication Theory*, *5*(3), 189-223.

Burns, P. (2016). *Entrepreneurship and small business*. Palgrave Macmillan Limited.

Yip, A. W., & Bocken, N. M. (2018). Sustainable business model archetypes for the banking industry. *Journal of Cleaner Production*, *174*, 150-169.

Santos, F., Pache, A. C., & Birkholz, C. (2015). Making hybrids work: Aligning business models and organizational design for social enterprises. *California Management Review*, *57*(3), 36-58.

Amit, R., & Zott, C. (2015). Crafting business architecture: The antecedents of business model design. *Strategic Entrepreneurship Journal*, *9*(4), 331-350.

Brau, J. C., Cardell, S. N., & Woodworth, W. P. (2015). Does microfinance fill the funding gap for microentrepreneurs? A conceptual analysis of entrepreneurship seeding in impoverished nations. *International Business Research*, *8*(5), 30.

Mahfuz Ashraf, M., Razzaque, M. A., Liaw, S. T., Ray, P. K., & Hasan, M. R. (2018). Social business as an entrepreneurship model in emerging economy: Systematic review and case study. *Management Decision*.

Karnani, A. (2016). *Fighting poverty together: rethinking strategies for business, governments, and civil society to reduce poverty*. Springer.

Cervantes, M., Lemus, D., & Montalvo, R. (2017). Implementing innovative financial models in different cultures: A comparative analysis of China and Mexico. *Cross Cultural & Strategic Management*, *24*(3), 508-528.

AirAsia

Background

Air Asia is often mentioned as the company that revolutionized budget aviation. Through unique idea of cutting cost and package sales, it paved it way through what was once considered to be the most expensive medium of transportation. The airline was established as a Malaysian corporation in 1993 and began its operations in 1996, whicht was created by a government-owned corporation, DRB-Hicom. With the airline being in debt, in December of 2001, AirAsia was purchased by Tony Fernandes of Tune Air Sdn. Bhd.

Air Asia structured as a low-cost airline; with headquarter is in Kuala Lumpur, Malaysia and operates scheduled domestic and international flights to 100 destinations across 22 countries. Its main hub for AirAsia is KLIA2 airport, the low-cost carrier terminal at Kuala Lumpur International Airport (KLIA) in Sepang area of Selangor, Malaysia. Its sister airline divisions are Thai AirAsia, Indonesia AirAsia, Philippines AirAsia, AirAsia Zest, and AirAsia India. AirAsia operates with the world's lowest unit cost of US$0.023 per available seat kilometers (ASK).

Business Model & Critics

The AirAsia declares its mission as following;

- To be the top company to work in, where employees are treated like family
- To create a globally recognized ASEAN brand
- To attain the lowest cost of any airline, so that everyone can fly with us
- To maintain the highest quality, to embrace technology, cost reduction, elevate service levels and provide our guests with a "WOW" experience

To commit to their vision, and by the end of 2006, AirAsia revealed a five-year plan to further improve AirAsia's presence in the Asian continent. Under the plan, AirAsia proposed enhancing its route network by connecting all of its existing destinations throughout the region and expanding further into Vietnam, Indonesia, Southern China

(Kunming, Xiamen, Shenzhen) and India, all of which are increasing markets in revenue and number of travelers.

Through its sister companies, Thai AirAsia and Indonesia AirAsia, the plan entails attention on developing its center in Bangkok and Jakarta. Increased frequency and the adding of new routes helped AirAsia to increase passenger volume to 17 million by 2017 fiscal years. AirAsia Thai is a joint project between AirAsia and Thailand's Asia Aviation. It attends the regularly scheduled domestic and international flights from Bangkok from its base in Suvarnabhumi Airport, Phuket and Chiang Mai. Currently, the AirAsia Thai fleet has 12 Airbus A320-200 and constantly increasing their air fleet while attempting to go public in the Thai stock exchange.

AirAsia Philippines opened in late December 2001, initially focused on international routes, gradually opening more local destinations to meet the booming economy. AirAsia X is focusing on long route businesses trips by focusing on business passengers, utilizing their airbus fleets A330, A340 and A350 XWB. Starting AirAsia X operations on 2 November 2007, its first service winged from Kuala Lumpur International Airport, Malaysia, to Gold Coast

Airport in Australia. AirAsia X travel within Asia, Oceania and Europe equipped by its 11 aircrafts. By early 2013, AirAsia's profits increased by 168% on a year-over-year basis amounting the airline's net profit at US$114.08 million. Although there was a 1% rise in the average fuel price, the airline managed to ear profits of 1.88 billion Malaysian Ringgit in 2012.

By executing several key strategies, AirAsia upholds its low-fare business concept. Among the most important approaches used is training programs, elaborated work practices and comprehensive risk management techniques. The airline realizes a high assets utilization concept by tumbling the turnaround time for their flights once they land in an airport to only 25 minutes, resulting high productivity rate. To meet the additional costs of their discounted services, passengers are provided with wide range of optional services that are available above the ground. Furthermore, the low-cost carrier business model of AirAsia is largely focused on the self-automation, cost-saving innovations, in addition to extensive networks and high frequencies of travel to their destinations.

AirAsia has a good management teams, with strong links to governments and stakeholders in various industries. By utilizing the diverse strengths of their executive management teams, Air Asia capitalize on the strengths of their management and continues to capture increasing market share. "Media friendly" has always been a strategic approach of AirAsia's management team, to dominate news chunks, along with the traditional print media advertising & promotions.

Sticking to their slogan "Now everyone can fly", the airline is dedicated to attract mass-market approach with prices appealing to everyone. One ground breaking feature of their business model is adopting e-commerce for ticket sales that proved very successful in engaging travelers, especially with younger consumers. On the other hand, including the complementary business opportunities like the accommodation service, a further add-on service compels the customer to pay more but see less. Partnering with other service providers like insurance, hotels and hostels, car rentals, hospitals (medical tourism), Citibank

(AirAsia Citibank card) formed unique opportunities for the company.

However, AirAsia does not have its own maintenance, repair and renovation (MRO) facilities. Initially, it may have been a better option to minimize their maintenance costs in order to ensure low-fare. But, with increasing number of aircrafts and increasing tours, AirAsia is forced to ensure appropriate compliance with international standard maintenance requirements, which may lower their overall maintenance cost in the long-run, rather than outsourcing MRO services. Air Asia has been receiving numerous complaints regarding various services issues, including wary vehicle conditions. Such complaints include flight delays, external or hidden charges to total tickets prices and the inability to change flights or get refund for reasonable causes as in the case of other airlines.

Critics argue that AirAsia consumer base is getting narrower with its inflexible policies. Most of customers and budget travelers need to plan their trip ahead of time. AirAsia's last moment prices tend to be on the high end. Additionally, service add-on and charges that are usually available for free at other airlines, along with small seats and non-free on flight food and beverages, makes AirAsia long distance journeys uncomfortable for passengers. Since the average income is rising throughout South-East Asia, more and more passengers preferring comfort and flexibility, rather than just being cheap ticket prices. AirAsia will need to restructure their business model and strategies as their size and business volume grows. Attention to changing consumer needs along with market forces will force changes in the very existence of the company to ensure servicing future mass-consumer base.

References

Ahmad, R. (2010). AirAsia. *Asian Journal of Management Cases*, 7(1), 7-31.

Alamdari, F., & Fagan, S. (2005). Impact of the adherence to the original low-cost model on the profitability of low-cost airlines. *Transport Reviews*, 25(3), 377-392.

Grant, R. M. (2016). *Contemporary strategy analysis: Text and cases edition.* John Wiley & Sons.

Shuk-Ching Poon, T., & Waring, P. (2010). The lowest of low-cost carriers: the case of AirAsia. *The International Journal of Human Resource Management*, 21(2), 197-213.

Lim, K. Y., Mohamed, R., Ariffin, A., & Guan, G. (2009). Branding an airline:: A Case STUDY OF AIRASIA. *Malaysian Journal of Media Studies*, 11(1), 35-48.

Lawton, T. C., & Solomko, S. (2005). When being the lowest cost is not enough: Building a successful low-fare airline business model in Asia. *Journal of Air Transport Management, 11*(6), 355-362.

Wensveen, J. G., & Leick, R. (2009). The long-haul low-cost carrier: A unique business model. *Journal of Air Transport Management, 15*(3), 127-133.

Burns, P. (2016). *Entrepreneurship and small business*. Palgrave Macmillan Limited.

Nair, S., Paulose, H., Palacios, M., & Tafur, J. (2013). Service orientation: Effectuating business model innovation. *The Service Industries Journal, 33*(9-10), 958-975.

SK-II

About the Brand

SK-II is a luxury skin care brand originated in Japan. Japanese scientists were looking into using natural ingredients into their products in the 1970s developed this skin care product. The skincare line was initially called "Secret Key" because the main objective was to find the secret to crystal clear skin. Benefits were found by using fermented yeast as the main ingredients for younger looking skin. It was told that the scientists observed the young looking hands of old people who worked at a *sake* brewery, and noticed the vast difference of their hands and their faces, which were old and wrinkly, but their hands were soft and smooth. The effect happens because women who worked at the brewery have been submerging their hands in fermented yeast for years. This theory was tested and proven to be true. As such, fermented yeast became the main ingredient for their best-selling product, which is called "Pitera" a *Facial Treatment Essence*. The essence is named as the "miracle water" that can transform any aging skin to more youthful-looking skin in just 14 days.

Business Model

With such success and being Japanese in time when consumers trust and value almost any Japanese product, in 1991, SK-II was bought over by the consumer goods giant Procter and Gamble (P&G). The bulk of SK-II's business is most certainly in Asia with Japan being its biggest market, however it is also sold in the US, UK and Spain and can be purchased in stores and online. SK-II is sold in departmental stores and is targeted to high-end customers who are willing to pay high price for their premium products. The starter pack costs about $45 USD while the *Age Protect Set* is priced at about $500 USD. This clearly shows that SK-II products are targeted the high-end market that can afford such expensive product and in quest for "younger looking skin", which can be found in their best-selling high-end priced products.

SK-II brand is known to use celebrities to advocate products and promote its uniqueness. The choice of celebrity is targeted towards the aged-group and mostly focuses on the "miracle water" product line.

Figure 2: Advertisement featured in magazines featuring brand ambassador Cate Blanchet

SK-II advertises heavily in women magazines that are focused on fashion, beauty and lifestyle such as *VOGUE*, *COSMOPOLITAN* and *INSTYLE* who has a very strong and mature women audience.

Controversy in China

Skincare companies are not without any controversies. Consumers, who are overly conscious or curious about the ingredient of a particular product, tend to spark a lot of controversies. This is exactly what happened to SKII back in 2006, when consumers in China found traces of neodymium and chromium, two ingredients that are banned in cosmetics and are known to be hazardous. The Guangdong Entry-Exit Inspection and Quarantine Bureau of China reportedly found that nine types of the brand's product contained the said chemicals and according to China's Regulations on Hygienic Standards for Cosmetics, cosmetics should not contain neodymium or chromium.

Health experts believed that neodymium can cause irritation of the eyes and if inhaled, can damage the lungs and the liver. Chromium is believed to cause skin diseases such as dermatitis and eczema. P&G, when asked about the status of the ingredients in their products officially released a statement defending the amount of the heavy metals found in the product as being safe and insignificant to the human heath. The official statement is conflicting with an employee's statement who was quoted saying that "…only a small batch of products suffered the problem.". The controversy prompted a fierce backlash from Chinese consumers and it made P&G withdraw all stocks of the shelves of the affected products, and stopped selling this particular line altogether to ensure reliability of other products they sale to customers during September 2006. The company was also forced to offer compensation to customers via refunds.

Back to Normal

The controversy made a huge impact on SK-II and P&G, largely because the Chinese market represents 4% of P&G's annual revenues and it is the fastest-growing market for skincare products. After a month-long suspension, P&G made an announcement that it would resume the sales of SK-II skincare cosmetics in the Chinese mainland. The announcement came after the General Administration of Quality Supervision, Inspection and Quarantine and the Ministry of Health, made a joint declaration regarding the safety of the brand's products and affirmed that neodymium and chromium detected in SK-II's products came from raw materials. The declaration confirms that the two dangerous materials do not exist in the products ingredients and they were brought in by raw materials. Products only posed a minor hazard to consumer's health if not used properly, and there have been no proved cases of health damage caused by tiny amount utilization of this particular product.

Going Forward

SK-II is a premium product targeted to high-end consumers who are willing to spend hundreds or thousands of dollars to gain a youthful look. Although SK-II has a strong loyal customer base, it tries hard to avoid controversies at all cost. When the news hit in 2006, consumers were scared to use the products because it might mess their faces, which is a primary concern for people. Numerous backlash on the Internet surfaced, with bloggers condemning the products and the issue headlined the news. The news came close to derailing the credibility SK-II has forged with consumers for more than 20 years. The news got the attention from consumer groups all over the world, and officials from other countries were urged by consumers to test the products as well.

A P&G spokesperson in America, when asked about the controversy that happened in China, avoided questions about P&G's credibility, but instead, highlighted the safety of SK-II's products saying, "…SK-II's products are safe and consumers can continue to use them with confidence. The situation in China is unique and is different from other countries…". Numerous governmental agencies around the world in charge of quality supervision of skincare and other products made announcement of the safe use of the product. P&G was quick to issue a statement that the SK-II products were safe without question.

Such move by P&G was regarded as too fast and arrogant by Chinese media, stating that the company has no respect towards nations' authorities. P&G quickly change its action by going into negotiations with government officials in China and decided to withdraw all of its products and offer refunds. Withdrawal of product is a costly affair to any company regardless of their size. However, such a move signals the notion that P&G cares about their consumer's safety and is willing to abide by Chinese rules and regulations. Refund is another costly activity that a company should avoid. However, in SK-II's case, refunding consumers showed that P&G a "Western Company" is honest and posses ethical values, contrary to what the news and authorities advocating. Such norms are highly regarded in Asian countries, which are known to hold deep cultural and human values. Finally, one controversy could not shake the strength of the SK-II brand, especially in the face of massive and swift response by a conglomerate such as P&G. Such efforts are still

216

ongoing to regaining consumers' trust in the Chinese market.

References

Bartlett, C. A., & Beamish, P. W. (2018). *Transnational management.* Cambridge University Press.

Huang, L. (2016). Electronic Words of Mouth in Facebook: A case study of SK-ll Facebook Fanpage.

Hyun, J. H., & Choi, S. B. (2018). Consumer purchase intention of a cosmetic product after the Fukushima nuclear incident. *Social Behavior and Personality: an international journal, 46*(4), 551-561.

Motohashi, K. (2015). Shiseido Marketing in China. In *Global Business Strategy* (pp. 155-171). Springer, Tokyo.

Schlegelmilch, B. B. (2016). Assessing Global Marketing Opportunities. In *Global Marketing Strategy* (pp. 21-41). Springer, Cham.

Chang, K. F., & Yang, H. W. (2016). What Are Product Bundles and How to Bundle Products. In *Let's Get Engaged! Crossing the Threshold of Marketing's Engagement Era* (pp. 135-139). Springer, Cham.

Roll, M. (2015). Transforming How We Understand Asian Cultures and Consumers. In *Asian Brand Strategy (Revised and Updated)* (pp. 37-68). Palgrave Macmillan, London.

Steenkamp, J. B. (2017). Customer Propositions for Global Brands. In *Global Brand Strategy* (pp. 45-73). Palgrave Macmillan, London.

Cervantes, M., Crimson, K., Figueroa, C., Hess, A., & Martinez, E. (2015). GM 105–12: PROCTER & GAMBLE COMPANY'S 2015 STRATEGIC AUDIT.

Schlegelmilch, B. B. (2016). Creating Global Product and Service Offerings. In *Global Marketing Strategy* (pp. 83-103). Springer, Cham.

NOVARTIS

ψ NOVARTIS

Company Background

Novartis International AG is **Swiss multinational pharmaceutical company** based in **Basel**, Switzerland. In 1996, Novartis came about as a result of a merger between Ciba-Geigy and Sandoz. Novartis and its predecessor company's origins can be traced back to more than 150 years of history in development of health care products. Beginning with the production of synthetic fabric dyes, then moving into producing chemicals, and eventually pharmaceuticals[1]. Novartis' board of Directors comprises of 11 members, with Joerg Reinhardt as the chairman. The board of Directors is responsible for the direction, strategy, organization and administration of the company. The board of directors have chosen Joseph Jimenez as the Chief Executive Officer (CEO) to lead and implement the company strategy.

Business Model

Novartis focuses its business on 3 leading divisions. They are; Novartis Pharmaceutical division, Alcon division, and

218

the Sandoz division. Novartis pharmaceutical is at the forefront of development and commercialization in oncology, primary care and specialty medicines. It develops innovative, patent-protected medicines to enhance health outcomes for patients and health-care providers. Alcon is a division focused mainly on eyes cares products. It has 3 businesses, which consist of surgical product, ophthalmic pharmaceutical and vision care. This division offers the world's widest spectrum of innovative eye care products that enhance the quality of life of patients. The third division is Sandoz, which is a global leader in the rapidly growing generics industry. 4 businesses Sandoz is focusing on are retail generics, biopharmaceuticals, oncology injectable and Anti-Infective. With Sandoz as a part of Novartis, it helps to make affordable, high-quality medicines available to more people.

Approach for sustainable growth

The way for a whole organization to sustain its business is through their sustainable growth. Of course Novartis' approach for sustainable growth is always with a focus on patients. To reach set goals of focusing on patients requires strategic alignment with their mission, vision strategies, and employees' buying into these values. Novartis' mission is "To Care and Cure". Charged with such mission, Novartis is able to discover, develop and successfully market innovative products to prevent and cure diseases, therefore easing suffering and to enhancing the quality of life.[1] The success of the mission thus far has encouraged Novartis' aim to be the world's most respected and successful healthcare company.

Norvatis has a series of strategies and plans for achieving its vision. The two strategies are; better patient outcome, and science based innovation. With these two strategies, it can bring the organization more focus and be more patient and innovation oriented. Better patient outcome mainly focusses resources on developing medicines and devices that can produce positive real-world outcomes for patients and healthcare providers. The benefits can range from improving the cost-effectiveness of high-quality care to prolonging lives. Novartis also develops services and technologies to augment the benefits of its core products such as diagnostic tools, smartphone applications to monitor patient health, and programs to help people lead healthier lifestyles.

For science-based innovation, Novartis maintains substantial investment in research and development aimed at areas of unmet medical need. The product pipeline is fed by a distinctive research and clinical approach that focuses on scientific advances before market potential. It is augmented by collaborations with academic researchers and other companies. [1] To lead in this area of healthcare, there are few values that was adopted to help achieve these objectives. These values are; innovation, quality, collaboration, performance, courage and integrity. These values helped Novartis to define their culture and to effectively execute company's strategies in line with their defined mission and vision. Novartis also set clear and standards and professional conduct that is expected of all their employees.

Business Model

Novartis is a global healthcare company based in Basel, Switzerland. It currently focuses on pharmaceuticals, eyes care products and generic medicine. Today, Novartis products are available in more than 180 countries worldwide. When assessing financial results of previous years, Novartis decided to perform a series of transactions.

The objective of the transaction is to make Novartis become more focused on core competencies and market opportunities, more profitable and help grow revenue streams. Due to increasing demand in the healthcare industry, Novartis acknowledged that only innovative businesses will maintain the lead in the industry, achieve global scale, and thrive in an increasingly competitive market. Novartis lead by the new CEO ran various analysis and came to the conclusion that their three main divisions (including pharmaceutical, Alcon and Sandoz) lack the scale to compete. However, the other three divisions; vaccines, animal health, and Over the Counter (OTC) tend to lack the needed innovation power and commercial scale to effectively compete. As such, Novartis management concluded that those three divisions, will not be able to compete effectively as a stand alone independent businesses.

Therefore, Novartis decided to reduce the number of independent divisions from six, to only three. In order to maintain Novartis global position as the world's number two company in cancer treatment, Novartis planned to acquire GlaxoSmithKline's (GSK) products. GlaxoSmithKline is a world leader in pharmaceutical products with state of the art research and development track record. By doing so, Novartis decided to sell its vaccine division, while giving the Influenza vaccine business to GSK. Such strategy, would not only benefit Novartis, but it would also be of benefit to GSK, since GSK's vaccines business has grown to become the world's largest vaccination company. After doing so, Novartis and GSK planed to merge their OTC business through joint venture. By doing so, the new merger would create the world's largest consumer healthcare companies. As a result of the merge, Novartis would own 36.5% of the joint venture.

In January of 2015, Novartis sold its Animal Health division to another global pharmaceutical company, Eli Lily. This transaction made Eli Lily the world second largest company in the animal health sector. Such set of actions as parts of a grand strategy, has contributed over the years to Novartis' core operational margins, as they became financially sound company. However, Novartis strongly believe that with the addition of GSK oncology products, focusing their investments in just three divisions and greater attention by senior management to operations is a driver for growth of future sales.

Challenges

Under the leadership of Jos Jimenez, Novartis is preparing to continuously transform itself. Such thinking is considered to be a formula for success. In the words of CEO Jimenez *"Over the next decade, we expect significant changes in healthcare. To prepare Novartis for a new phase of growth, we sharpened our strategy and transformed our company."*. Understanding the power of demographic shifts taking place in their markets as the world's population is projected to increase by nearly 1 billion people by 2025, half of which are expected to be over 50 years old. People over 50 years old are in high need of medical attention and pharmaceutical solutions. As such, demand for healthcare is inevitably increasing as the world population increase. This is expected to place greater strain on governmental and family budgets, but will provide greater opportunities to companies like Novartis. New technologies and investments in research and development will pave the way for new treatments and medical breakthroughs that will help the global population. To succeed in the new competitive pharmaceutical environment, each segment of the industry must be competitive enough through constant innovation and value creation to effectively compete. Novartis revenues by the end of 2017 jumped to $22.87 billion USD.

References

1. www.novartis.com/news/publications/annual-report-2017
2. Boulet, L. P., FitzGerald, J. M., & Reddel, H. K. (2015). The revised 2014 GINA strategy report: opportunities for change. *Current opinion in pulmonary medicine*, *21*(1), 1-7.
3. Jahnke, W., Bold, G., Marzinzik, A. L., Ofner, S., Pellé, X., Cotesta, S., ... & Stauffer, F. (2015). A general strategy for targeting drugs to bone. *Angewandte Chemie International Edition*, *54*(48), 14575-14579.
4. Furrer, O. (2016). *Corporate level strategy: Theory and applications.* Routledge.

ZALORA

Company background

Based in Singapore, ZALORA is a subsidiary of ZALORA Global Fashion Group, founded in 2012 by "Rocket Internet GmbH" with a capital of $238 million USD. Rocket Internet is the largest online startup incubator and some of its other ventures that have a presence in South East Asia are FoodPanda and Wimdu. Zalora has a presence throughout South-East Asia; Malaysia, Singapore, Indonesia, Philippines, Thailand, Vietnam, in addition to Hong Kong and Taiwan. To date, Zalora is the largest and fastest growing fashion e-commerce sites and Asia's leading online fashion retailer. [1]

Business Model

Zalora offers an extensive online collection of men's and women's clothing, shoes, accessories, and beauty categories. Brands range from local to international names.

ZALORA's business model is to create a shopping experience that is "easy and fun". Zalora has been very active in their market, helping vendors throughout South-East Asia to create their own "branded storefront" utilizing ZALORA platform. This set up help vendors maintained their branded storefront with the support of ZALORA. Such oversight and assistance, is handled by ZALORA account manager. [2]

ZALORA's approach to their business model is as following;

1. Easy navigation:
   ZALORA online store enjoy a simple layout and user-friendly interface, that is easy to navigate, through guided step-by-step process.

2. Safe shopping experience:
   With safety being the the primary reasons that Asian consumers avoid online shopping. ZALORA utilizes multiple secure payment options to provide safe payment system environment to their customers. Safe payment methods include; invoicing payment, direct debit payment, prepay

payment, cash-on-delivery payment and credit card payments. Once a customer is charged through one of the payment options available, the customer is informed about the status of their purchase and receives a tracking number for follow up on delivery.

3. Quick shipping experience:

    Making sure that sold items are shipped and delivered within 1 to 3 working days.

4. Free delivery with minimum purchase and free return within 30 days:

    Depending on the country of purchase, the Free delivery and free return is intended to be taken advantage of for customers with a minimum amount spent, which can also qualify them for free delivery. This policy of improved shipping experience allows customers to make returns within 30 days of receiving the order.

5. Commitment to consumer through customer service support:

    A customer service support team is dedicated via live-chat or hotline to answer customers' questions, track orders and deal with any issues may arise.

Zalora is facing an increasing competition from diverse competitors and online fashion sellers. Fashion Valet and 11 Street, is just an example of the increasing online shopping for fashion throughout Asia. To secure their position in the marketplace, Zalora came up with number of solutions to meet the increasing competitive landscape.

1. Focus on mobile commerce [5]

   Traditionaly, Zalora has been able to reach consumers via search engines and focus on Facebook. Building on their internal research, which has shown that over 45 percent of the company's sales come from mobile devices (app and mobile site). As a result, since 2014, Zalora moved their attention to focus more and more on mobile commerce. This action began with major improvements to their iOS and Android applications. Zalora also find it feasible to capitalize on such strategy by partnering with the popular messaging application in Asia "Line" a mobile commerce shopping service, to provide special offers, discounts and other offers.

2. Taking the online store offline [5]

Not uncommon strategy with many online services providers, Zalora started to offer convenience store pick-ups in Thailand, as an option for their customers at over 7,200 branches of the very popular store "7–11". To their surprise, the store pick-up option did not succeed as they thought it would, this is primarily because of the fact that more than 50 percent of e-shoppers prefer to pay using cash on delivery (COD) system. The pick-up service option at 7-11 doesn't allow for cash on delivery. As a result, Zalora thought they should solve this problem by providing convenience stores with COD option. Once customers are able to pay for their packages at 7–11 stores, such solution would be more appealing to customers since 7-11 tends to be everywhere in Thailand. Setting up actual stores and "pop-up" shops across South-East Asia is an essential component of Zalora's plans to move from online to offline, now that their brand name is known amongst customers. Such stores will function as showrooms, whereby customers are able to try out fashion offered, however, orders must be made made online.

3. Provide more diverse options for customers [5]
    To diversify their fashion portfolio, Zalora started in Singapore to offer their own new fashion label called "Ezra".

4. Reaching out to first-time buyers [5]
    Knowing that the online fashion shopping business is still a green field with plenty more room for all vendors to compete and grow, Zalora is capitalizing on the opportunity of gaining more market share by getting more first-time buyers.

Summary

Online shopping and e-commerce markets in South East Asia is still growing and has not matured yet, unlike markets in the U.S. and Europe, where Amazon and eBay has a majority of the market sales and where other big retailers such as Walmart are paving a share for themselves in that market. Zalora's approach based on their strategic actions to the marketplace is capitalizing on the opportunity of an emerging marketplace. With number of small vendors, increasing disposable income, Internet savvy consumer, increasing middle-class with desire for shopping for trendy fashion, Zalora is poised to increase their presence through larger market share, providing more value on investment to their shareholders Rocket.

References

1. "About Us". Archived from www.zalora.com.my on 25 December 2015.

2. Mishra, Pankaj. "Rocket Internet-Backed Fashion Site Zalora To Launch Marketplace In Asia". 14 January 2014. Tech Crunch.

3. Lunden, Ingrid. "Rocket Internet Fashion Group GFG Raises $35M, Poaches Amazon Exec To Lead It". 9 April 2015. Tech Crunch.

4. Ho, Victoria. "Rocket Internet-Backed Fashion Portal Zalora Launches iOS App, No Word Of Android Yet". 24 April 2013. Tech Crunch.

5. Wong, Crystal. "6 tactics Zalora is using to beat the fashion ecommerce competition". 18 June 2014. Techniasia.

6. Cunningham, Susan. "Rocket's Lazada And Zalora Lost $235.3 Million In 2014 But Are Moving Toward Profitability". 12 May 2015. Forbes.

7. de Vasconcellos, I. M. P., & Monteiro, H. S. E-COMMERCE BUSINESS MODEL STRATEGY OPPORTUNITIES AND CHALLENGES IN BRAZIL.

8. Abdullah, S. S., & Hilman, H. (2015). E-Strategy Adoption and Implementation: Re-examining the Concept. *ADVANCES IN GLOBAL BUSINESS RESEARCH Vol. 12, No. 1, ISSN: 1549-9332*, 723.

9. Shia, B. C., Chen, M., Ramdansyah, A. D., & Wang, S. (2015). Comparison of decision making in adopting e-commerce between

Indonesia and Chinese Taipei (Case Study in Jakarta and Taipei City). *American Journal of Industrial and Business Management*, *5*(12).

10. Hariandja, E. S., & Afsari, M. U. GROWTH STRATEGY FOR E-COMMERCE USING DIGITAL MARKETING: A Case Study of Brodo.

11. Sulaiman, F. M., & Hidayat, N. K. Analysisof Value Creation Towards Business Performance: a Case Study of a Local Brand "The Little Things She Needs.".

12. Faeni, R. P. (2016). Influence of Pop Culture, Emotional Trust, Inconsistent Reviews and Consumer Purchase Intention on Zalora's Women Product in Indonesia. *Scholedge International Journal of Management & Development ISSN 2394-3378*, *3*(2), 20-31.

Sanofi Aventis

Company Background

Sanofi-Aventis is a French pharmaceutical conglomerate firm based in Paris. Sanofi-Aventis engaged in pharmaceutical research and development, manufacturing of medicinal and therapeutic solutions that meets patients' needs. Sanofi-Aventis portfolio covers a wide range of therapeutic products ranging from cardiovascular and diabetes care to rare diseases and oncology, immunology, generics, to consumer healthcare. Such product line makes them one of the largest human vaccination producers. By 2014, Sanofi-Aventis was the world's fifth largest pharmaceutical company by sales revenue [4].

The long history of Aventis in pharmaceuticals and healthcare, dates back to 1718, when a family of pharmacists founded Laboratories Midy. Sanofi on the other hand dates back to 1973 as subsidiary of Elf

234

Aquitaine and Synthélabo. Sanofi was founded in 1970, as a result of merger of two French pharmaceuticals, Laboratoires Dausse, which was founded in 1834, and Laboratoires Robert & Carrière (1899). In 1973, the French cosmetics giant L'Oréal in an attempt to diversify their portfolio, found an opportunity by acquiring the majority of Sanofi shares. Meanwhile, Synthelabo acquired Laboratories Delalande in 1991.

In 1999, Sanofi-Synthelabo was formed as a result of merger between Sanofi and Synthelabo in France. During that time, Sanofi was ranked as the second largest healthcare company, while Synthélabo was ranked as the third largest pharmaceutical group in France. However, such history of takeovers and mergers resulted in Sanofi-Synthelabo acquiring Aventis through a hostile takeover in 2004, creating Sanofi-Aventis [5]. After a series of lawsuits by consumers and controversies, the board decided to simplify the name of the company from Sanofi-Aventis, to Sanofi. The attributed such a board decision to making the name easier to pronounce, particularly to Chinese consumers.

Business Model

Over the past few years, Sanofi has taken a few strategic decisions that have gained them a leading position in the pharmaceutical industry. The growth of Sanofi is the result of strings of mergers and acquisitions (M&A) of competitors, something that proved to be a strategically advantageous to Sanofi. Additionally, Sanofi invested heavily in R&D knowing that finding new drug or cure will place them ahead of their rivals. Such strategies asserted Sanofi's market position globally and their dominance in key segments of the pharmaceutical industry, such as generics and vaccines.

Revenue of Sanofi from 2006 to 2017 (in million euros)

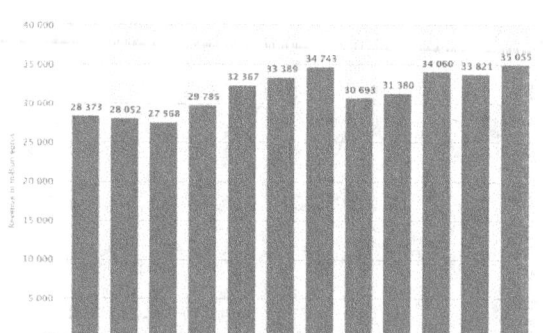

Source: https://www.statista.com/

As a result of such strategic planning, Sanofi has organized itself into seven growth platforms, with emphases on growing segments of the global market such as; diabetes, vaccines, consumer healthcare, Genzyme, animal health, and other products that are expected to be of high demand in global Markets. Such position and organization structure has been the result of replacing former CEO *Chris Viehbacher* in late 2014 with new CEO *Olivier Brandicourt*. The new CEO Mr. Brandicourt wanted to streamline operations into five business units; diabetes & cardiovascular, specialty care such as; rare diseases, multiple sclerosis...etc., general medicines and emerging markets as matured portfolio [8].

The new and simplified structure is meant to drive growth through improved market position. such structure is meant to be aligned with new plans of introducing new medicine, every six months between 2016 and 2018[6]. This strategy comes in response to an increasing pressure to cut cost from governments, generic drug since patents tends to expire within 10 years, and any drug makers can copy their drug, which may cost in billions of USD in research and development. Sanofi redefining its priorities also attributed to the changing nature and transformations in the pharmaceutical industry. The new structuring by

237

diversifying portfolios is also seen as a new positioning of the company to face an increasingly competitive environment. The idea behind the new restructuring is to position Sanofi in a way that increases organizational agility, and streamlined operations in a way that can increase innovative solutions across several pharmaceutical and health care areas, and ensure sustainable competitive advantage and growth.

Conclusion

The realignment of R&D streamlining with production capacity and tighter control over sales and marketing expenses, has helped Sanofi to manage the impact of patent loss of their bestselling medicines that cost them billions in R&D to develop and market. In the years to come, with Sanofi's new business strategy, the outlook of the firm looks positive they are expected to continue to grow and innovate, while focus on key market segments to strengthen their position in the industry amongst rivals.

The restructuring plans they are undergoing, focused on simplifying the company structure and drive long-term growth, has shown positive results. This is something illustrated in their annual revenues shown in the diagram above. Moreover, one major fact to note is that with several products in the company's portfolio is now off patent, which opens the door wide open for every manufacturer to copy the drug and mass market it, there is a pressure on Sanofi to maintain sales and revenue with existing top products. The company needs accelerate the development of products in the pipeline, and be the first to market new medical solutions to remain competitive in their industry.

References

1. "Annual Report 2014" (PDF). Sanofi-Aventis. Retrieved 26 November 2015.
2. "Annual Report 2013" (PDF). Sanofi-Aventis. Retrieved 26 November 2015.
3. "2015 Sanofi in a Glance" (PDF). Sanofi- Aventis. Retrieved 27 November 2015
4. Tracy Staton for Fierce Pharma. 18 March 2015 Top 15 pharma companies 2014 revenue.
5. Muller-Stewens, G. and Alscher, A. (2006). The Acquisition of Aventis by Sanofi. St. Gallen Institute of Management, 1-15.
6. Gen News. 15 July 2015. Sanofi Shrinks Business Units to Five in Restructuring.
7. Robert Wiesman for Globe Staff. 15 July 2015. Genzyme Will Expand, Take a New Name.
8. Zacks Equity Research. 16 July 2015. Sanofi Unveils Restructuring Plans, Prunes Business Units.
9. Matthias Blamont and Noelle Mennella for Reuters. 15 July 2015.

239

Sanofi Announces Reorganization Ahead of Strategic Plan

10. Sanofi Website. Accessed 25 November 2015

11. Trivano. 6 November 2015. Sanofi Sets Out Strategic Roadmap for Long-term Growth.

ICICI BANK

Company Background

ICICI Bank Ltd. is a major banking and financial services institution based in India. ICICI Bank Ltd was incorporated in the year 1994 as a part of the ICICI group with the name ICICI Banking Corporation Ltd. The initial equity capital was 75.0% by ICICI and 25.0% by SCICI Ltd. A result of the merger between SCICI, and ICICI. ICICI Bank became a wholly owned subsidiary of ICICI. In 1999, the name of the Bank was changed from ICICI Banking Corporation Ltd to ICICI Bank, only to make it the second largest bank in India, with the second largest market capitalization in India with total revenue of $ 128 billion USD. ICICI Bank offers a wide range of banking products and financial services, ranging from corporate to retail banking, utilizing a variety of delivery channels and through their specialised subsidiaries. Areas of investment are; banking, life and non-life insurance, venture capital and assets management.

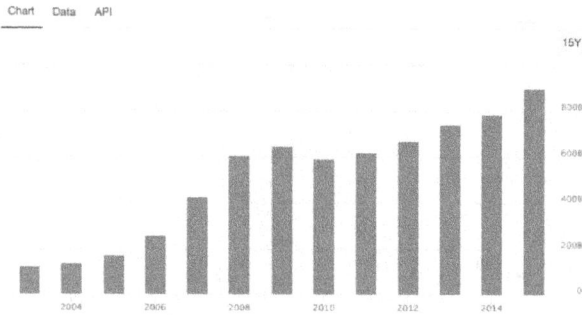

Annual Revenue: Billion in Indian Rupee
Source: https://tradingeconomics.com/icicibc:in:sales

Business Model

The Bank used both organic and traditional growth strategies. To get around the difficulty of branch licensing, ICICI used acquisition as a strategy to increase their branch networks. For instance, they acquired Bank of Madura, Sangli Bank and the Bank of Rajasthan. As of 2017, ICICI bank has over 2,550 branches as part of their network, and over 6,301 ATMs throughout India. ICICI bank operates in 18 countries in addition to India. ICICI'S banking business model is based not only on serving their primary market segment, but to gain as much of the low-income rural

242

market as possible. They see low-income rural market as an opportunity to grow and developed commercial and retail subsidiaries [1]. To that end ICICI has implement three primary strategies to penetrate rural area. This is done by defining distribution points, prepare rather than react to the increasing rural market, and to support distressed communities and treat them as viable markets.

The above strategies are aimed at uplifting the poor in the country through participation in the rising economic activities India undergoing, and for the decades to come. The management team view the rural market segment as growing with great potential, since 30% out of over 500 million bank account deposits belong to the rural population. The bank reports that only 18% penetration was attained of the 746 million rural population. [1]

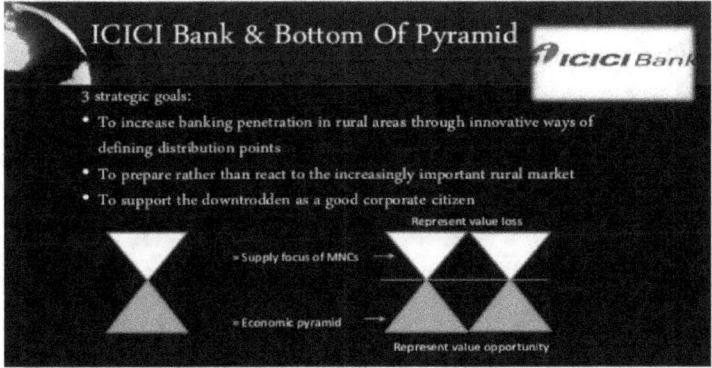

Since ICICI focused their banking attention on the bottom of the economic pyramid (see the figure above) they created microfinance financial solutions for low-income households. This is primarily because such market segment in India is not well served, and because it's a growing segment for most banking and financial institutions in developing economies.[2] ICICI reports that only one million households have an access to microcredit, and therefore, there is plenty of room to grow.

ICICI have increased their banking presence in rural areas through increase of the number of available distribution points. To minimize expansion cost, ICICI formed partnership with NGOs and other microfinances institutes as third party service providers. Other actions taken as cost reduction measures are; piggybacking on established contacts, and implement two innovative models. The first is *Direct Access Bank Led Model,* by which merging with other rural banking institutions such as Bank of Madura. This is a significant move, because Bank of Madura has significant presence in Southern India's rural areas. With customer base of 1.2 million, and 77 branches, such joint venture will provide wider access to rural markets. The second model is *Indirect Channel Partnership,* whereby they leverage the relationship with rural organizations, to expand presence and accessibility to their services, and avoid costly expansion process.

Mechanism of the strategy

Bank of Madura's developed *Self Help Group* (SHG) and implemented this program during 1995, by which, training and initiation of small groups of women to undertake financial activities in banking, saving and lending proved to be effective by providing them with credit facilities. By 2000, they had created around 1200 SHGs across Tamil Nadu geographical area. SHG program had been successful in several states throughout India; yet, such program was limited only to those areas where branches are available. The partnership model of ICICI Bank was aimed at reaching out to those areas, where the bank did not have branches and as a result, no services may be provided.

Through this partnership with Bank of Madura, ICICI Bank saved on initial costs of business development rural areas. They where able to create infrastructure of network through other parties and service providers that offers micro credit

245

distribution channels, to take advantage of existing and available expertise of other institutions serving rural areas.

Competitive Advantage

Additional actions take by ICICI is coming up with the theme of "khayaal aapka" or "Thank you". In this theme, ICICI have rolled out 27x7, 365 days' electronic branches. These electronic branches serve as access to internet-banking using debit-card, cheque deposits, and 24 hours' video conferencing facility to communicate with customer care. Additional actions taken by ICICI is the availability of secure banking from within Facebook account for any Facebook user, and offering Money2India, Tab banking, iBizz as examples of innovative products and services offered to customers. Leading the industry by thinking constantly about customer's convenience is what differentiates ICICI from other competing banks (4-traders, 2013). Today, ICICI Bank (NYSE:IBN) stands to be India's second largest bank and largest private sector bank in India, with assets of over $43 billion USD. [1] ICICI was the first bank to offer Internet banking services in India. They are extending online banking services to various rural communities via kiosks to expand on their reach of customers.

According to the managing director and CEO Mrs. Kochhar[1][2] the cornerstones of ICICI Bank's digital strategy that helped place the on top of others is based on three key pillars. These are, digital, mobile and social, capitalizing on digital platform, and extending service via mobile and social media platforms, whereby younger generations tends to spend significant amount of time on such platforms.

ICICI Bank continues to expand their microfinance services through 100,000 additional agents. ICICI continue to encourage growth through direct sales agents to further push microfinance products into more rural regions of the Indian sub-continent. Services offered in rural areas include plans to provide farmers with credit from sugar companies, seed companies, dairy companies, NGOs, micro-credit institutions and food processing industries. Another way of increasing their presence in rural areas is launching mobile ATM services. ICICI Bank branded trucks started going around rural areas and villages with ATMs on board. [1][2]

Challenges

In response to bad loans, or as they describe it "unclaimed loans" which rose up to 3.40 percent in December of 2014, tend to be an issue to all banks and lenders. ICICI Bank is putting in place a special entity to deal with bad loans called Stressed Assets Management Group. Learning from State Bank of India that managed to deal with Non Performing Assets (NPA) successfully. Although ICICI enjoys wide presence outside of India, yet most companies abroad rather do business with stable and reputable global banks such as HSBS and Citi Bank. So as far as global expansion, it is not an area of strength for ICICI and something they should not focus on at the moment.

Conclusion

The Bank used both organic and traditional growth strategies. With over 2,550 branches as part of their network, and over 6,301 ATMs throughout India, Growth strategy for ICICI and business model is based on gaining as much of the low-income rural market as possible. As they pursue low-income rural market as an opportunity to grow and developed commercial and retail subsidiaries, the three primary strategies to penetrate rural area are; defining distribution points, being prepared rather than reacting to the growth of rural market, and to support distressed communities and treat them as viable consumers.

The above strategies are aimed at uplifting the poor in the country through participation in the rising economic

248

activities India undergoing, as growth potential in rural India is promising 30% of the Indian market, which consist of over 500 million bank account deposits. ICICI has numerous quality issues to deal with both in India and abroad. However, they will not be able to compete globally unless they improve the quality of their personal and operations to match those of competing global banking brands.

References

1. ICICI Bank Report 2017. Retrieved from https://www.icicibank.com/aboutus/annual.page?
2. http://forbesindia.com/article/big-bet/chanda-kochhar-making-icici-banks-digital-strategy-click/41159/1#ixzz3v8UwA600
3. Neilson, L. C., & Chadha, M. (2008). International marketing strategy in the retail banking industry: The case of ICICI Bank in Canada. *Journal of Financial Services Marketing, 13*(3), 204-220.
4. Goyal, K. A., & Joshi, V. (2012). Merger and Acquisition in Banking Industry: A Case Study of ICICI Bank Ltd. *International Journal of Research in Management, 2*(2), 30-40.
5. Parameswar, N., Dhir, S., & Dhir, S. (2017). Banking on innovation, innovation in banking at ICICI bank. *Global Business and Organizational Excellence, 36*(2), 6-16.
6. Ilyas, S. (2015). DECODING INDIA'S UNIVERSAL BANK-A PERFORMANCE ANALYSIS OF ICICI BANK. *ASBBS Proceedings, 22*(1), 225.
7. Prabhu, G. G., & Chandrasekaran, G. (2015). A Comparative Study on Financial Performance of State Bank of India and ICICI Bank. *Jurnal ilmiah Research Sains. International Journal of Research in Business Management (IMPACT: IJRBM) ISSN (E).*
8. Agarwal, T. (2016). An Analysis of the Twin Pillars of the Banking in India: Financial Literacy and Financial Inclusion. *Gavesana Journal of Management, 8*(1/2), 23.
9. Jose, S., & Chacko, J. (2017). Sustainable development of microfinance customers: An empirical investigation based on India. *Journal of Enterprise Information Management, 30*(1), 49-64.

10. Kelkar, U., James, C. R., & Kumar, R. (2015). The Indian insurance industry and climate change: exopsure, opportunities and strategies ahead. In *Climate Change and Insurance* (pp. 66-79). Routledge.
11. Parameswar, N., Dhir, S., & Dhir, S. (2017). Banking on innovation, innovation in banking at ICICI bank. *Global Business and Organizational Excellence*, *36*(2), 6-16.
12. Singh, S. (2016). Impact of Digital Marketing on Indian Rural Banking.

NETFLIX

Netflix started in 1997as a DVD mail order rental service. Driven by story telling according to the CEO, today, they evolved their business model into video streaming the world largest streaming service company turning them into the world largest entertainment company. By 2022, they are expected to spend $22.5 billion USD on content such as movies and TV programs in different languages, changing and contributing to the growth of the global entertainment industry.(1) Unmatched by any of Hollywood studio companies, in 2018, Netflix is financing 84 movie production to provide as original content on their entertainment platform.

Netflix serves 125 million households around the world (except China) through a fixed monthly subscription. This number is double the number of households they served in 2014. With an average household watching about 2 hours a day of their favourite programs on Netflix, which is customizable per family members preferences and targeted recommendations. This global demand for Netflix service constitutes one fifth, or about 20% of the global bandwidth download stream. This is because Netflix customers are mostly outside the United States rather than within the US market. As such, they are redrawing the economics and norms of TV watching, turning it into entertainment on demand. With such diverse consumer base, they have the luxury of diversifying content offering and not limiting their investments into one type or one language of TV programs or movies.

Such business model would not have been possible without faster Internet, which left most media and entertainment studios with plenty of catching up to do, which is difficult since Netflix has a first mover advantage and grown a market and consumer base that generates enough revenues to to maintain the production of new programs that meets the thirst of their subscribers. This success is expected to generate revenues equivalent of more than half of the current income of entertainment studios in the United States. By chasing the global consumer, they are expected to grow even bigger in the coming years.

References

Goldman Sacks, The Economist, June 30,2018 edition.

Gomez-Uribe, C. A., & Hunt, N. (2016). The netflix recommender system: Algorithms, business value, and innovation. *ACM Transactions on Management Information Systems (TMIS)*, 6(4), 13.

Jenner, M. (2016). Is this TVIV? On Netflix, TVIII and binge-watching. *New media & society*, *18*(2), 257-273.

Adhikari, V. K., Guo, Y., Hao, F., Hilt, V., Zhang, Z. L., Varvello, M., & Steiner, M. (2015). Measurement study of Netflix, Hulu, and a tale of three CDNs. *IEEE/ACM Transactions on Networking*, *23*(6), 1984-1997.

McCord, P. (2014). How netflix reinvented HR. *Harvard Business Review*, *92*(1), 70-76.

ABOUT THE AUTHOR

Firend Alan Rasch Holds a Ph.D in applied management and decision science (USA). Dr. Rasch is a prominent scholar and expert in Southeast Asian region. His experience as investments banker with major banks in California, United States, provides an insight into various industries of the Silicon Valley. Worked as Sr. Management Consultant with McKinsey & Company, KPMG, and Anderson Consulting advising U.S. Fortune 500 companies. Co-founded Micro-Fuzz Technologies, a start-up that was sold later to IBM. Lectured in numerous countries including USA, Korea, Malaysia, Qatar, UAE, and now the UK, in the field international marketing, Entrepreneurship, Innovation & Technology. 20+ years of experiences in international business, combining both East and West, his insight and interpretation of current and future markets outlooks are of importance to marketers and policy makers in Southeast Asia and an active researcher in the fields of global management and international business activities.

OTHER BOOKS BY THE AUTHOR

For Citation, please cite as following: Firend, Al. R.

Find out more books by the author at Amazon:

- Critical success factors in project management: A comparative study between the GCC and the U.K.
https://www.createspace.com/7607885

- Employability and learning: strategies to improve students capacity: Essay of educator reflections
https://www.createspace.com/7545335

- Asian Case Studies: Lessons from Malaysian Industries, (2016) ASIN: B01LXLWX2I
https://www.amazon.com/s/ref=nb_sb_noss?url=search-alias%3Dstripbooks&field-keywords=Asian+Case+Studies%3A+Lessons+from+Malaysian+Industries

My Academic Blog: http://drfirendblogs.blogspot.com

Additional references used in this book

Andrew McAfee, Brynjolfsson, E. 2017 *Machine, Platform*, Crowd: Harnessing Our Digital Future. W. W. Norton & Company; 1 edition

BMIMatters. (2012). *Understanding google business model.* Retrieved 12 6, 2015, from http://bmimatters.com/2012/03/29/understanding-google-business-model/

Carlson, N. (2014). *The story of how larry page got forced from the top of google and came back a decade later.* Retrieved 12 4, 2015, from http://www.businessinsider.my/larry-page-the-untold-story-2014-4/?r=US&IR=T#qXJkWORbcWMjOJbU.97

Google and the Fundamentals of Internet Business. (2010). *Google business model.* Retrieved 12 3, 2015, from https://sites.google.com/site/net205apples/google-business-model

Krawczyk, K. (2014). *Google is easily the most popular search engine, but have you heard who's in second?* Retrieved 12 4, 2015, from http://www.digitaltrends.com/web/google-baidu-are-the-worlds-most-popular-search-engines/

Neal, R. W. (2013). *Google partners with facebook: Internet advertising rivals agree to help each other grow ad revenue.* Retrieved 12 3, 2015, from http://www.ibtimes.com/google-partners-facebook-internet-advertising-rivals-agree-help-each-other-grow-ad-revenue-1434374

Steegle. (n.d.). *Google 101 facts: 76-101 google's amazing work culture.* Retrieved 12 5, 2015, from http://www.steegle.com/about/google-101-facts/76-101-googles-work-culture

AAPL Investors.net. (2014). *Mergers & acquisitions.* Retrieved December 26, 2015, from http://aaplinvestors.net/stats/acquisitions/

all about Steve Jobs.com. (n.d.). *Timeline.* Retrieved December 27, 2015, from http://allaboutstevejobs.com/bio/timeline.php

CBS News. (2014, July 23). *Is apple too dependent on the iphone?* Retrieved December 26, 2015, from http://www.cbsnews.com/news/apple-stock-dependent-on-iphone-6-success/

Clark, D. D. (2009, April 10). *Apple incorporated.* Retrieved December 27, 2015, from http://www.appstate.edu/~eb74040/Documents/Research/ApplePaper.pdf

Cranford, H. (2013, April 6). *A swot analysis of apple.* Retrieved December 26, 2015, from http://beta.fool.com/hjcranford/2013/04/06/a-swot-analysis-of-apple/29418/

Maha. (2012, December). *Critical analsis of using marketing strategies of branding apple inc.* Retrieved December 26, 2015, from http://www.slideshare.net/sweetNsourr/dissertation-25988438

McCormack, F. (2013, October 27). *Apple's iphone marketing strategy exposed.* Retrieved December 26, 2015, from https://smallbusiness.yahoo.com/advisor/apple-iphone-marketing-strategy-exposed-032350605.html

Mittan, S. R. (2010, January 28). *Apple: a case study analysis.* Retrieved December 27, 2015, from http://homepages.wmich.edu/~gershon/courses/4480/APPLE%20-%20A%20Case%20Study%20Analysis%202010-01-28.pdf

Shadyramadan. (n.d.). *Mac os history.* Retrieved December 26, 2015, from http://www.timetoast.com/timelines/mac-os-history--2

Strategic Management Insight. (2014). Retrieved December 26, 2015, from Apple swot analysis 2014: http://www.strategicmanagementinsight.com/products/swot-analyses/apple-swot-analysis-2014.html

The Telegraph. (n.d.). *Mac at 30 timeline: apple's every major product.* Retrieved December 27, 2015, from http://www.telegraph.co.uk/technology/apple/10580156/Mac-at-30-timeline-Apples-every-major-product.html

Time. (2014, February 13). *Relax: apple innovation is fine*. Retrieved December 26, 2015, from http://time.com/8040/relax-apple-innovation-is-fine/

Rosoff, M. (2015, August). *What is alphabet, google's new company?* Retrieved December 12, 2015, from http://www.businessinsider.my/what-is-alphabet-googles-new-company-2015-8/?r=US&IR=T#KuMFO9scgd1hE7Js.97

Titcomb, J. (2015, August). *Google and alphabet: What does this all mean?* Retrieved December 12, 2015, from http://www.telegraph.co.uk/technology/google/11796103/Google-and-Alphabet-What-does-this-all-mean.html

Amazon Com Inc. 24 March 1997. Nasdaq. Retrieved
Byers, Ann (2006), Jeff Bezos: the founder of Amazon.com [PDF], The Rosen Publishing Group, pp 46.
Rivlin, Gary. "Retail Revolution Turns 10". 10 July 2005. New York Times. Retrieved.
Layton, Julia. "How Amazon Works". 25 January 2006. HowStuffWorks.com. Retrieved December 15, 2011
Noren, Eric. "Analysis of Amazon Business Model". 9 July 2013. Digital Business Model.
Stone, Brad. " Amazon, The Company that Ate The World". 28 September 2011. Bloomberg. Retrieved
Mordoukoutas, Panos. "What's Wrong with Amazon's Business Model''. 27 October 2014. Forbes. Retrieved
Amazon Web Services Launches Amazon EC2 for Windows". Amazon.com. 23 October 2008. Retrieved May 27, 2014.
"Amazon plans big expansion of online grocery business: sources". Reuters. 4 June 2013.
Friedman, Mara (2004). Amazon.com for Dummies [PDF] Wiley Publishing. R
Olsen, Stefanie. "Amazon invests in Engine Yard's cloud computing". 14 July 2008. News.cnet.com. Retrieved August 4, 2011.
Robert Spector (2002). Amazon.com: Get Big Fast.

ROBERTSON, D. (2014) BRICK BY BRICK: HOW LEGO REWROTE THE RULES OF INNOVATION AND CONQUERED THE GLOBAL TOY INDUSTRY

How Apple's Business Model Burned Samsung
https://techpinions.com/how-apples-business-model-burned-samsung/35093
SAMSUNG VS. APPLE: COMPARING BUSINESS MODELS
http://www.investopedia.com/articles/markets/110315/samsung-vs-apple-comparing-business-models.asp
Samsung Electronics Co., Ltd. Sales Preparation
http://www.hoovers.com/company-information/cs/sales-preparation.Samsung_Electronics_Co_Ltd.a166cb2c88a2e408.html
Samsung Electronics
http://www.samsung.com/us/aboutsamsung/
Business Model Analysis (Part 1) – Samsung
http://www.academia.edu/5611981/Business_Model_Analysis_Part-1_-_Samsung

2014 SAMSUNG ELECTRONICS ANNUAL REPORT
http://www.samsung.com/common/aboutsamsung/download/companyreports/2014

Shimizu, N., and Takeuchi, H. (n.d.). The Contradictions That Drive Toyota's Success

http://www.toyota-industries.com/corporateinfo/history, Retrieved on 23rd November 2015.

http://www.huawei.com/en/about-huawei
http://www.huawei.com/en/about-huawei/annual-report
http://www.ft.com/intl/cms/s/0/c67364e2-d1f9-11e3-8ff4-00144feabdc0.html#axzz3vynW9E7n
http://www.huawei.com/en/
http://www.androidcentral.com/these-are-top-huawei-phones-you-need-know
http://www.spiegel.de/international/business/the-secret-ways-of-little-known-chinese-telecoms-giant-huawei-a-875297.html
http://www.theglobeandmail.com/report-on-business/international-business/asian-pacific-business/in-global-smartphone-battle-chinas-huawei-steps-up/article18128776/

http://www.huawei.com/en/publications/winwin-magazine/vr-or-nothing

http://www1.huawei.com/en/about-huawei/corporate-info/research-development/index.htm

http://carrier.huawei.com/en/

http://consumer.huawei.com/en/mobile-phones/

http://www.worldairlineawards.com/awards/world_airline_rating.html

http://www.qatarairways.com/my/en/ceo-message.page

http://www.qatarairways.com/my/en/csr.page

https://en.wikipedia.org/wiki/Qatar_Airways

https://www.qatarairways.com/iwov-resources/temp-docs/press-kit/Qatar%20Airways%20Factsheet%20-%20English.pdf

http://apex.aero/2015/10/20/qatar-airways-ceo-akbar-albaker-ifec

http://www.qatarairways.com/global/en/press-release.page?pr_id=pressrelease_osaka-suspension-301115&locale_id=en_gl

http://www.qatarairways.com/global/en/press-release.page?pr_id=pressrelease_011215_nagpur_start

http://www.traveldailynews.com/news/article/69108/qatar-executive-ndash-first-private

http://www.justhere.qa/2015/11/qatar-duty-free-qatar-museums-open-new-store-cafe-hamad-international-airport/

https://www.digitalnewsasia.com/startups/11street-goes-live-in-malaysia?page=2

https://simple.wikipedia.org/wiki/11street_Malaysia

http://www.kpopstarz.com/articles/196200/20150427/lee-minho-met-with-fans-in-malaysia-as-11street-brand-ambassador.htm

http://www.businesscircle.com.my/11street-bets-big-on-malaysia/

http://www.marketingmagazine.com.my/breaking-news/11-000-for-11street-rm35m-invested-in-malaysia

http://www.koreatimes.co.kr/www/news/biz/2008/04/123_19653.html

http://www.ukessays.com/essays/marketing/market-position-analysis-for-TATA-motors-marketing-essay.php#ixzz3tcVdSql1

http://www.ukessays.com/essays/marketing/TATA-motors-a-business-strategy-report-marketing-essay.php#ixzz3tcKFFCtc

http://www.thehindu.com/business/Industry/TATA-motors-investing-strongly-in-products-and-technologies-to-be-futureready-mistry/article7434704.ece

ISBN-13: 978-1721060603
ISBN-10: 172106060X